HAUS CURIOSITIES

Not for Patching

About the Contributors

Frank Field has been MP for Birkenhead since 1979. In 1997–98 he served as the Minister of Welfare Reform and is now Chair of the Work and Pensions Select Committee.

Andrew Forsey is Frank Field's Senior Parliamentary Researcher and served as Secretary to the All-Party Parliamentary Inquiry into Hunger in the United Kingdom.

Frank Field and Andrew Forsey

NOT FOR PATCHING

A Strategic Welfare Review

First published by Haus Publishing in 2018
4 Cinnamon Row
London SW11 3TW
www.hauspublishing.com

A CIP catalogue record for this book is
available from the British Library

Print ISBN: 978-1-910376-79-9
Ebook ISBN: 978-1-910376-80-5

Typeset in Garamond by MacGuru Ltd

Printed in Spain

Contents

Preface

"A revolutionary moment in the world's history is a time for revolutions, not for patching"[1]

– Sir William Beveridge, 1942

A paradox. Elections can be decided by the amount of taxpayers' money each political party believes should be spent by the government. Yet, for so long, the total sum of taxpayers' hard-earned cash going to each of the major government programmes, and particularly the largest – the welfare budget encompassing health, social care, social security, education, and housing – has been unclear to most of the country. Equally strange is how little attention has been given to what those programmes have achieved with that cash. Our aim is to ignite a debate on what outcomes taxpayers seek from those sums of money. In doing so, we seek to persuade the reader that the government should set up a strategic welfare review, just as successive post-war governments began to regularly produce strategic defence reviews.

Now, we believe, is an opportune moment to begin a new relationship between the government, as collector of taxes, and taxpayers, who are often resistant to paying them. We believe a strategic welfare review could play a crucial part in gaining attention, building understanding, and winning support among taxpayers for a certain level of taxation that would be clearly linked to agreed objectives of policy around the theme of a good society. To borrow a part of Bentley Gilbert's description of the early architects of the welfare state, this major political innovation would, in respect of the social evils that afflict our society, 'settle the lines upon which the eventual solutions could be found'.[2]

This way forward suggested itself after reading Peter Hennessy's *Distilling the Frenzy*, in which he recalls the emergence of the post-war strategic defence reviews.

Defence of the realm is the primary purpose of government. Of this goal, and the means of financing it, taxpayers have had an extraordinarily benign view. Threats to our national security have remained high during much of the post-war period, but defence – the size of its budget and how such a budget is spent to achieve national security – has hardly troubled the scorers in any poll that gauges taxpayers' concerns over how their money should be used.

Even in the age in which we now live, of unprecedented multifaceted terrorist, chemical, and cyber threats – in addition to what defence policy has traditionally set out to achieve – taxpayers' attitudes to what the size of the budget should be to meet these threats remains amazingly becalmed.[3] And even when the country has not directly been involved in military conflict, the regular strategic defence review has retained its status as a cornerstone of government policy in pursuit of national security.

Not so with other forms of public expenditure, particularly the welfare budget. Here, we attempt to pick up the Hennessy challenge apply to the welfare budget the approach that has become standard practice in the strategic defence reviews.

In this first attempt to present a case for a strategic welfare review, we have largely focused on three items of expenditure – health, social care, and social security – and largely excluded education and housing, as well as the range of the powers that the Treasury has to affect living standards. Not because the latter are unimportant. Far from it. Rather, because we aim to make this first stab at a strategic welfare review manageable for authors outside the government machine.

Any attempt at meeting the Hennessy challenge will need to factor in a whole range of variables: the number of people contributing to the welfare budget; the number of people drawing support from the benefits and services financed by it; the willingness of the country to pay a certain level of contributions in pursuit of certain outcomes attached to those benefits and services; changes in family size and composition, as well as developments in the labour and housing markets; and the use of new technologies and techniques in the delivery of benefits and services, to name but a few.

We argue in this volume that the task of initiating a regular strategic welfare review is the only feasible means through which taxpayers and the state can seek to navigate a clear path through these variables. It would do so by pulling them together into a single ongoing consideration of our country's needs and the ability to meet them under different circumstances in the years ahead.

Indeed, it is this approach that is being taken by the National Infrastructure Commission. Since its creation in 2015, the commission has been tasked by the government with producing a National Infrastructure Assessment once in every Parliament, setting out its assessment of our country's long-term infrastructure needs, conducting in-depth studies into the most pressing infrastructure challenges, and monitoring the government's progress in delivering infrastructure projects and programmes recommended by the commission.

The Low Pay Commission has taken a similar approach, since it was established in 1998, to determining the government's immediate and longer-term labour market policy. Its job is to provide independent advice and recommendations to the government, based on meticulous research and analyses of underlying trends in the economy, around matters relating to statutory minimum wage rates. It has been asked in recent years to recommend rates for the National Living Wage such that it will reach 60 per cent of median earnings by the end of this decade, subject to its own assessments of the state of the economy.[4] For other statutory minimum wage rates, it has been asked to recommend increases to help as many low-paid workers as possible, without damaging their employment prospects. The success of this strategy is evident in the relatively substantial growth, particularly in recent years, in both the hourly wages as well as weekly earnings of the low paid.[5]

In seeking to apply this approach to the welfare budget, we are immediately faced with a second paradox. A great deal of the information necessary for such an analysis on health, social care, and social security is published in stops and starts by the Office for Budget Responsibility. But the important work of this organisation is not built up, at present, into a comprehensive plan for the welfare budget that is approved by the Cabinet and then debated seriously in Parliament.

We are only too aware that to make the strategic welfare review comprehensive we would need to consider all actions of government affecting living standards, in particular within education and housing, as well as the role of the Treasury.

We seek in this volume to awaken public debate and demonstrate that the government should commit itself to the first of what would become regular strategic welfare reviews, thereby kick-starting any necessary changes in the machinery of government to achieve the objectives set out in each review, just as the early post-war governments began a process that has now led to the regular production of strategic defence reviews and the reorganisation of the government machinery required to implement them.

With the UK leaving the EU, there could not be a more

fitting time for the government to heed Sir William Beveridge's salient call to action – this is not a moment for patching – and set out what it believes to be the country's social objectives and how they ought to be paid for over the coming decades. A strategic welfare review could play a crucial role in giving the country a new sense of purpose and direction. We are the last to pretend that such a task is easy; it is quite the opposite. But such an exercise will never be achieved unless a government has the courage to begin the task.

Introduction

In this short volume, *Not for Patching: A Strategic Welfare Review*, we call for a major revolution by the government to bring together, under a strategic welfare review, six elements that will form the basis of a new social contract:

- the total expenditure on what we call the welfare budget: health, social care, and social security in the first instance, followed by education and housing;
- the objectives that taxpayers seek from this expenditure;
- the changes in the machinery of government required to meet these objectives;
- the costs of meeting these objectives over time against the best estimates of what the demand will be, population growth, changes in technology (particularly for health and social care services), and changing public attitudes to the size of the welfare budget;
- the options for meeting these costs; and
- a comprehensive set of data on specific outcomes so that taxpayers can demand a regular report back on how successfully their money has been spent by the government.

As things stand, the terms of that social contract – the duties bestowed upon taxpayers and the government in pursuit of a certain quality of life for all of this country's citizens – are as unclear as they are unsettled. While they remain so, we will have failed as a country to confront the social evils of today, let alone reach a longer-term settlement for securing the welfare of future generations.

Hence the importance of a major revolution to bring together these different factors under a strategic welfare review. It is from the findings of this exercise that the government of the day could negotiate with taxpayers over a set of clearly defined objectives for the welfare budget and its constituent parts, as well as how the costs of achieving those objectives are to be met and how the machinery of government will need to change for them to be met.

Two important staging posts on the quest we set the government in respect of the welfare budget – by far and away the largest part of its spending of taxpayers' money – were marked in 1958.

The first was the publication by the Macmillan government of its *Central Organisation for Defence*, the first such document to be published since 1946. *Central Organisation for Defence* was a short, fourteen-paragraph publication that marked one of those seismic changes in how the government believes it should act in fulfilling its primary purpose of protecting its citizenry. The publication helped to set the tone for a series of what have become known as strategic defence reviews.

Fourteen paragraphs of *Central Organisation for Defence* may have been presented to the public, but Prime Minister Macmillan had also been energetic in enforcing the disparate organisational parts of his government responsible for spending the defence budget. It is here that serious consideration began to be given to, first, what the projected needs were to protect Britain in a fast-changing world, and, second, what organisational changes in government had to be made to achieve these objectives.

The second pioneering publication came from the pen of the Cambridge economist John Vaizey, also in 1958.[6] Vaizey's ever-curious mind was struck that although the first taxpayers' grant towards the costs of educating the population was made in the 1830s, and universal education was enforced in 1870 by the Education Act, nobody could report with any accuracy on the total size of the education budget (divided between local and national government), let alone on whom it was spent.

And so began the long haul to publish comprehensive data on the size and disbursal of the education budget.

We still have a long journey before we can sensibly answer all the questions taxpayers may pose on how their money is spent. We do not know, for example, the administrative and organisational structure of how the education budget should look in ten years' time to give every child the best start in life, and how this budget will be interlinked with each and every part of the welfare budget's objectives and expenditure. Such questions around the interlinked determinants of our national security are addressed through the regular production by the government of strategic defence reviews. No such equivalent exists on the national welfare front.

Herein lies another paradox. When Macmillan made his call to arms over the organisation of our nation's defence, its budget constituted 7.6 per cent of national income. It is now a mere 2 per cent of Gross Domestic Product (GDP). And yet the financing and organisation of the defence budget is regularly subject to a rigorous review, most recently so in the *National Security Capability Review* of 2018. In contrast, the welfare budget, on which we call for the beginnings of regular strategic reviews, has risen over the same period from 16 per cent of national income to 25.6 per cent of GDP.

This call to action on the national welfare front, similar to the one that Prime Minister Macmillan made on the national security front sixty years ago, will entail a major exercise, but one we believe can be achieved in stages.

Computing the comparable data will be the easiest part of the task. We then need to consider how these budgets will grow and on what assumptions those growth rates are made. Setting out these assumptions on growth patterns could be seen as a highly political act. But these sets of data need to be linked with the equivalent data on outcomes that these expenditures will deliver.

Courage will be required to begin an open dialogue with voters on how the existing budget projections will be met from taxpayers' pockets, as well as how existing budgets can be better spent, or, failing that, the consequences of cutting services in nominal and maybe real terms if taxpayers are unwilling to sign up to a new social contract.

It is that dialogue we seek to open in the chapters that follow.

A call to arms

Governments have decided on four separate occasions in the post-war period – 1946, 1958, 1963, and 1984 – to publish accounts titled *Central Organisation for Defence*, detailing the findings of an exercise carrying the same name. The sole focus of this exercise, as stated in 1958, was on 're-shaping and re-organising the armed forces in accordance with current strategic needs and in the light of the economic capacity of the country.'[7]

A more frequent exercise running alongside the publication of *Central Organisation for Defence* papers has been that of the strategic defence review which looks regularly at levels of expenditure and manpower, against a backdrop of changing threats to our national security as well as our ability to repel them within certain financial constraints. As Peter Hennessy notes, 'all of these reviews had a strong element of cost-push behind them and a desire to reduce the proportion of GDP absorbed by defence. Aspirations were perpetually outstripping resources.'[8]

The Attlee government, in great secrecy, conducted the first such review at the beginning of the post-war period. The Harwood review on the shape and size of the armed forces, which reported behind closed doors in 1949, sought to limit the annual defence budget to an average of £700 million over the three years between 1950 and 1952. By the end of that three-year period, the Churchill government had devised its strategy for countering the threat of the Cold War.

Five years later, the Sandys review brought about a strategic shift in resources to bolster our nuclear deterrent, at the expense of more conventional military means.

Two reviews were set up by Denis Healey in the 1960s, as the state again tried to tighten its belt and cut defence expenditure by cancelling a series of major equipment orders. In line with their main objective of reducing the share of GDP spent on defence, the Healey reviews' key recommendation was to shrink the size of Britain's global footprint.

Later, the Mason review of 1975 looked set to tighten the government's belt still further, with the objective of cutting the proportion of GDP spent on defence – from 5 per cent to 4.5 per cent within a decade – by reducing the total size of our manpower by 11 per cent. The main objective was to prioritise resources for NATO and the country's nuclear deterrent in countering the threat posed by the Soviet Union.

Likewise, the Nott review of 1981 foresaw drastic reductions in the Royal Navy's surface fleet and a prioritisation of ground forces for NATO, as a means of freeing up resources for the country's nuclear deterrent and achieving the stated objective of bringing defence procurement in line with a certain level of resources. The Falklands War put paid to such plans.

The next review, *Options for Change,* offered up a new strategic vision for the post–Cold War era. Published in 1990, it ushered in further cuts to the size of the army, air force, and navy. This was to continue into the *Defence Costs Study* of 1994, which, while reorganising command structures and pushing for more joint operations, foresaw a reduction in the number of Armed Forces personnel of 18,700 by 2000.

The emphasis of the Blair government's *Strategic Defence Review* in 1998, as well as its *New Chapter to the Strategic Defence Review* in 2002, was on both increasing the number of joint operations and trying to determine how many overseas operations the UK could conduct at any one time with or without our allies.

The coalition government's *Strategic Defence and Security Review* in 2010 was the first post-war review to look at not only our military capabilities, but also counterterrorism, overseas aid, manning our borders, and cyber security.

Taking into account a similar exercise undertaken by the Cameron government in 2015, there were twelve post-war strategic reviews of the defence budget and manpower, conducted in the light of events overseas and financial constraints at home. These reviews were begot by falling real budgets at a time when governments wished our country to play an overactive role in international affairs, given our resources.

What has been the overall impact of the regular strategic defence review on government policy and expenditure? The process has surely been effective, particularly in the reorganisation of existing resources and manpower to adapt to changing threats, while the whole defence budget has been reduced as part of the total government budget, and as measured by its proportion of GDP.

Looking more broadly at how this process could be applied to other areas of public expenditure, we identify three clear lessons for establishing an effective strategic welfare review.

The first lesson is the obvious one. The whole exercise depends on the collection of the necessary data, including long-term projections. One example here is the publication of an annual defence equipment plan that is based on the Ministry of Defence's planned spending on equipment for the next decade. The National Audit Office then publishes its analysis of that plan.[9]

The second lesson is that, like the strategic defence review, a strategic welfare review's objective must be to bring about meaningful change. This objective necessitates institutional reform. The establishment of a similar body to the National Security Council (NSC) is needed to drive through the objectives linked to a strategic welfare review.

The NSC is the main forum for collective discussion of the government's objectives for national security and about how best to deliver them. A key purpose of the NSC is to ensure that ministers consider national security in the round and in a strategic way. It necessarily meets weekly and is chaired by the Prime Minister, with four ministerial sub-committees covering specific areas of national security. We believe a similar structure to the NSC is needed to drive forward a strategic welfare review, even if the meeting schedules may be much less frequent.

A third lesson is the linking of taxpayers' money to specific objectives, as to the most effective use of the government budget. This lesson is drawn from a much more recent reform instituted by the May government.

One of the most ambitious post-war reviews of our national security capabilities occurred in July 2017, when the National Security Adviser was asked by the May government to lead a review of the changing nature of the threats posed to the country, across twelve areas of security. Once it had identified those threats, the review assessed the capabilities the country could draw upon to meet them. It then set out the reorganisation of the government machinery required to enhance our capabilities, as well as the levels of resources the government would need to commit to the maintenance of our national security on each front. Appended to the document was an update on the implementation of the Cameron government's review of 2015, so that taxpayers could gain a clearer understanding of how effectively or otherwise their monies had been spent on this front.[10]

Crucially the review covered not only the budget commanded by the Ministry of Defence, but all of those budgets that our country would call upon to counter security risks in the years ahead. If our national welfare is to be similarly secured, a strategic welfare review will necessarily begin by incorporating the combined total budgets for health, social care, and social security. Other budgets need to be included over time, such as education and housing, and particularly expenditure on the first crucial years – the Foundation Years – of a child's life.

We would expect to see the structure of the two most recent reviews of our national security apparatus replicated in a strategic welfare review, thereby bringing about a revolution that clearly ties monies spent to specific objectives. One example from the May government's security capabilities review is of 'our £2 billion investment in the Special Forces [that] will ensure they are best configured for overseas and domestic tasking'.[11] Three other examples, from the Cameron government's review, are the pledges to 'invest £1.9 billion over the next five years in protecting the UK from cyber attack and developing our sovereign capabilities in cyber space';[12] to 'do more to ensure our security and intelligence agencies have the resources and information they need to prevent and disrupt plots against this country at every stage' by investing 'an additional £2.5 billion, including employing over 1,900 additional staff and strengthening our network of counter-terrorism experts in the Middle East, North Africa, South Asia and Sub-Saharan Africa';[13] and to increase 'from £1 billion in 2015/16 to over £1.3 billion a year by 2019/20' the Conflict, Stability and Security Fund, which, under NSC direction, 'provides a greater link between strategic decision-making and action on the ground, and in directing cross-government departmental effort in fragile states'.[14]

A strategic welfare review would also need to consider what changes are required in the configuration of the government machinery to achieve a clear set of social objectives; what this reconfiguration will mean for the levels of resources and manpower required within each part of the welfare budget to achieve those objectives; how we can regularly monitor and report progress to taxpayers on each front; how we do so across departments within a single strand of work; and what pitfalls need to be avoided if such logic is to be applied successfully over time across the whole of the welfare budget.

Strategic defence reviews have been aimed primarily at cutting expenditure and then trying to balance the defence of the realm within that reduced budget. Clearly there is a debate to be had on whether that same overall force for change will dominate a strategic welfare review, or whether the size of the welfare budget will in fact grow more rapidly, rather than reduce, as a result of this ongoing exercise.

A dominant characteristic of all strategic defence reviews – trying to have more than one's cake, as well as eating it – is likely to apply to a strategic welfare review. Each of the strategic defence reviews is marked by a demand from the Treasury to cut expenditure, while at the same time using fewer resources more effectively in maintaining Britain's defences, as well as the command the country has on the international stage.

We have learnt from the strategic defence review that there is a need for the government not only to bring together the necessary data, which clearly is the first and most basic task for a strategic welfare review, but also to commit to the implementation of the outcomes of the review by constantly developing its own machinery so that the objectives of policy can be delivered. The national security objectives set out in each strategic defence review have been driven through largely by changing the machinery of government. Such a change in the government's machinery will be necessary both in the collection of data for a strategic welfare review and in achieving the objectives to which expenditure has been designated.

The time is long overdue for this approach to be taken to the welfare budget. The capabilities, as well as the vulnerabilities, of our society require an open and ongoing assessment. The task of determining and setting aside the resources to guard against those vulnerabilities must then follow. As must any rigorous changes in the organisation of services required to achieve such objectives.

Ensuring the organisation of our defence meets our national security needs is a pivotal role given to the NSC. We believe that an equivalent body should be established, as one of the first steps in building up a strategic welfare review and driving through its policy recommendations.

One-off reviews have already been attempted within different parts of the welfare budget. We survey, in the following chapters, their impact on government policy and expenditure.

Back to Beveridge?

In the post-war period, there have been dozens of one-off reviews, Green Papers, and White Papers covering social security, social care, and health. As the Institute for Government has noted, the aim of such reviews 'is normally to lend independent credibility to a plan, depoliticise an issue or build cross-party support for policy proposals'. They can also 'provide political cover for a government to implement potentially unpopular policies and can increase the likelihood of a proposed solution lasting in the longer term'.[15]

We briefly analyse a selection of those reviews here, for they contain important lessons for building up a more comprehensive, overarching strategic welfare review. Before doing so, we look at the closest thing this country has had to an all-embracing review – the Beveridge Report of 1942.

Crucial to the underpinning of our national welfare is the setting of national minimum standards below which no service or income is allowed to fall. Sir (later to become Lord) William Beveridge was the first social reformer ever to set out a comprehensive social plan detailing a new minimum income floor for all who were out of work, and forecasting the cost of maintaining that floor over two decades. This was to form part of Beveridge's co-ordinated assault on the 'five giants' of want, ignorance, squalor, idleness, and disease. What is surprising is that, seventy-six years on, we are still far from achieving this minimal goal for the whole of the welfare budget, as the following story recalls.

Sir Kenneth Stowe, who was a long-serving private secretary in the civil service, recalled in 1988:

> I've been in and around [the benefits system] for 36 years and I never heard anybody seriously suggest that we should set up a scientific study to discover what the adequate basis for [benefit levels] is to be. There were no real reviews of adequacy [of benefit levels]. The Social Security Review initiated under Norman Fowler did not address adequacy. It took the framework as it was and started necessarily from the standpoint of cost.[16]

Although there was an internal review of benefit adequacy conducted within the National Assistance Board in the early 1960s, its findings were never published and no further attempt to test the adequacy of benefit levels, or even to set minimum standards, has been made by any government since.[17]

Sir Kenneth's remarks raise two important questions. First, how efficient are single one-off reviews at changing the course of policy? Second, as with defence, to what extent have those reviews been driven largely by the desire to cut costs, rather than prioritising an effort to meet human need?

Our attempt at answering each question begins with a brief visit back to Beveridge, from whose review of social security we draw three themes to guide the work of a strategic welfare review.

First, in the paper summarising Beveridge's review for the War Cabinet, ministers were presented with estimates of the level at which benefits would need to be set if the objective of protecting the poor from destitution was to be achieved. Those subsistence rates formed one of Beveridge's 'six principles'[18] of social security, which themselves rested on 'three assumptions' for the rest of the welfare budget.[19] The six principles were also to guide Beveridge's recommendations on the reorganisation of the government machinery, with a package of responsibilities being transferred into a new Ministry of Social Security.

Second, as part of this comprehensive review of social security, Beveridge set out how expenditure would increase overall, as well as on individual items within this budget, between 1945 and 1965.

Third came Beveridge's recommended means of financing that increase in expenditure – 'whatever money is required for provision of insurance benefits should come from a Fund to which the recipients have contributed'.[20] For this he set out detailed recommendations on how the costs of paying benefits at certain rates would be met by contributions to the National Insurance Fund from individual households, employers, and the Treasury.

With these three moves, Beveridge prepared the ground for what could easily have been shaped into a regular strategic welfare review. Indeed, this course of action was recommended to the wartime government by Sir George Epps, the Government Actuary at the time, who argued for an actuarial review of Beveridge's plan to slay the 'five giants' to be made at regular intervals.[21] Yet no government ever picked up the ball and ran with it.

Instead, as we show later, one-off reviews have been conducted mainly in search of budgetary cutbacks or administrative tweaks within individual parts of the welfare budget. But they have failed to engage with a broader consideration of how our country is to secure the welfare of its citizens in the longer term. Here, two further lines of enquiry, stemming from Beveridge, gain pertinence.

First is the extent to which the administration of today's social security system and the government's policy by which it is guided are capable of bringing periods of little or no income to an end as soon as possible – or whether, in fact, both the administration and policy are prolonging those periods, exposing poorer households to the destitution that Beveridge was determined to see consigned to the pages of history.

The War Cabinet was briefed on how Beveridge saw social security primarily to mean 'security of income up to a minimum, but the provision of an income should be associated with treatment designed to bring the interruption of earnings to an end as soon as possible'.[22] Clearly the longer people are without an adequate income, and worrying about how they will stave off hunger or homelessness without digging themselves deeper into debt, the less time and energy they have to either look for, or stay in, work.

Shouldn't a main objective of the welfare budget be to help people without money get on the right benefit as quickly and safely as possible? The speed and accuracy with which the welfare budget is administered, to guard against our country's vulnerabilities, is one of the outcomes that must feature in an overall strategy – as the 2018 review of national security capabilities noted, 'rigorous implementation' is 'essential'.

Why then does the current government's flagship welfare policy, Universal Credit, go totally against the grain of such an approach, thereby destroying the living standards of the most vulnerable households?

The National Audit Office has found that 67 per cent of Universal Credit claims submitted by households with limited capability to work are not paid in full or on time, i.e. after five weeks. The same is true for 24 per cent of claims submitted by poorer households seeking help towards their housing costs, 23 per cent of claims from households requiring help to raise disabled children, 32 per cent of claims in which households are applying for help towards their childcare costs – a vital lifeline for low-paid workers – and 24 per cent of claims from households containing unpaid carers.[23]

The government has responded to the concerns raised around the plight of these households, in the main, by piling even more debt onto their shoulders. That debt takes the form of loans called 'advance payments'.

In doing so, it has ridden roughshod over the moral economy of the working class. The repayment of these loans, alongside any other outstanding debts, begins as soon as Universal Credit is finally in payment. Four recent examples of the impact of this policy and its administration come from Wirral's food banks: a man in his late 50s was reduced to tears when almost £200 was deducted from his monthly Universal Credit payment of £300 – he could barely afford any food or fuel, and fell into rent arrears; a young woman needed to use a food bank after £60 – almost a third of her Universal Credit payment – was deducted; another claimant was reduced to hunger after their whole month's Universal Credit was snatched away to repay debt on an 'advance payment'; and a fourth person sought urgent help after £180 was deducted from their monthly payment to repay historic social security debt.

A key lesson from Beveridge is that, on these trends, and in the absence of a strategic welfare review that sets national minimum standards, Universal Credit will help to transform the welfare state from one which protects people from poverty to one that drives them into destitution.

What role could a strategic welfare review take on, in

protecting claimants as well as taxpayers, with respect to the treatment of social security debt and repayments? According to the National Audit Office, the government currently has no estimate of the extent to which problem debt leads to increased use of public services, or the resulting cost to the taxpayer, while the available evidence shows that good debt collection practices both benefit individuals and boost collection rates. Moreover, the government lags behind other sectors in following good debt management practices.[24] An immediate task for a strategic welfare review, therefore, would involve undertaking such a task, as well as identifying on the back of this analysis where and how debt collection and management practices can be improved across government.

We in no way underestimate the comprehensiveness of the Beveridge review in trying to underpin a minimum standard of living for each individual in this country. However, a second line of enquiry in the strategy for which we advocate stretches beyond the Beveridge review, which made no attempt 'to deal with other social provisions such as housing, education or industrial welfare'.[25] These challenges have a huge bearing on people's living standards.

A necessary part of a strategic welfare review, therefore, will be to develop the role of the state and the other great powers of the land in effectively meeting these challenges. What moves are required to prevent the poor health outcomes and restricted life chances, for example, that arise from inadequate conditions in the labour and housing markets, as well as the education system?

We look next at attempts throughout the post-war period to 'deal with' different parts of the welfare budget, as well as the statistical, political, and methodological lessons that will need to be applied through a strategic welfare review.

Back to Phillips?

There have been six significant reviews of the social security budget in the post-war period.[26]

The first was commissioned by the Churchill government in the early 1950s. It was chaired by Sir Thomas Phillips, the first Permanent Secretary to the Ministry of National Insurance. In the light of potential deficits in the National Insurance Fund arising from an increase in the size of the pensioner population, the Phillips Committee was asked to review the economic and financial problems of providing for old age.

Clearing the way for the government to chip away at Beveridge's plan for social security in old age, the Phillips Committee spelled out how:

> [...] pension expenditure at present rates will rise two and a half times as fast as the number of elderly persons; [...] in the near future, even assuming no increase in the rates of benefit, there will be a deficit in the working of the [National Insurance Fund] and this deficit will grow rapidly. It is likely to be £126 million in 5 years' time, and £364 million in 25 years' time. No provision is at present made for meeting these deficits [...].[27]

The government accepted uncritically the Phillips Committee's key recommendations for downgrading the role of the contributory National Insurance pension in providing social security in old age and, instead, for means-tested National Assistance benefits to be given an increasingly significant role in bringing pensioner incomes up to an adequate minimum level.

This intellectual grip to which governments subjected themselves throughout the post-war period – that the contributory National Insurance pension would never be able to provide an adequate minimum income – was busted by Adair (later to become Lord) Turner's major review of the state pension, which reported to the Blair government and, beyond that, helped to shape the reform programme of the coalition government. Alongside a national auto-enrolment scheme to boost levels of saving in occupational pensions, a new state pension was to be phased in at a level that secured an adequate minimum income, and universal coverage was to be achieved by significantly reducing the number of contribution years required to receive it, as well as ensuring that people outside the labour market would be able to qualify without needing to rely on means-tested top-ups. We come back to the breaking of that mould later in this chapter.

Returning to the Phillips Committee's work, and in search of a structure within which a strategic welfare review could fit, we would draw the reader's attention to two particular features. First, it highlights, as became increasingly obvious during the post-war years, the rise in the numbers of retired people compared to the numbers in work. Second, the report touches on a growing concern in today's politics – the need not merely to consider how a state pension can be financed, but also how people in advancing years have to draw on health and social care. In this respect, the Phillips Committee acted as a true prophet.[28] Yet its thinking on this front was not fully expanded or acted on by the government.

A third feature is also worth examining. The Phillips Committee identified 'two major issues that emerge from this analysis: a) what can or should this generation do to ease the task of the next in providing for the elderly? b) what can a future generation afford to do for the elderly out of its own resources without undue strain?', before going through each of the variables that would determine the answers to these questions – the level of contributions, scope of coverage, the level of the state pension age, the size of annual increases, pension rates, and private pension provision. This was followed by an attempt at gauging the scale of the increase that was to occur in the ratio of pensioners to the working population.

A lesson for us is that major determinants of future financing may not be easily discernible and addressed unless there is regular updating in strategic welfare reviews, which are of course partially concerned with how the unexpected sneaks up and overpowers us. It is Donald Rumsfeld's 'unknown unknowns' that are the real devils in defeating rational policy, but which could be overcome by a regular strategic welfare review.

The second significant post-war review of social security came a quarter of a century after the Phillips Committee, in 1978, when the government switched its focus to benefits paid to those below the retirement age. The key recommendation from that review, titled *Social Assistance: A Review of the Supplementary Benefit Scheme in Great Britain*, was for the system of means-tested support to be simplified, reducing the level of discretion, and thereby made less costly.

What followed five years later was the third significant exercise – the Fowler review established by the Thatcher government – covering pensions, housing benefit, benefits for children and young people, and supplementary benefit. The result of the review was a Green Paper and then a White Paper heralding the twin substitution of income support for supplementary benefit, and family credit for family income supplement, as well as the halving of the value of the State Earnings Related Pension Scheme.

Another decade was to pass before Peter Lilley, as Social Security Secretary, commissioned two analyses of trends in social security expenditure – *The Growth of Social Security* and *Containing the Cost of Social Security: The International Context* – which would form the fourth significant review.

It is in the structure of this review, although not necessarily its conclusions, that we see the basis of a review of the welfare budget in the round:

> [...] we have embarked on a fundamental review of the social security programme. The aim is to improve the system: to make it better focused to protect the vulnerable, to ensure that we all have the means to cope with the needs and contingencies of modern life and to make sure the system does not outstrip the nation's ability to pay. I want to encourage a constructive national debate on how these objectives can best be achieved. Such a debate needs to be based on the facts. How has the system grown? What factors are driving its development? What influences particular benefits? How likely is it to grow over the rest of the century and beyond? This document aims to provide the information needed to answer these questions [...] it is inevitable that spending on the elderly will increase as the number of people over retirement age will rise sharply in the first three decades of the next century. The message that underlying growth in social security has exceeded, and will continue to exceed, growth in the economy is an uncomfortable one. But it must be faced. There are bound to be different views on the appropriate size of the programme and on who should benefit and by how much.[29]

There are a number of important lessons in these two quotations that are significant for any strategic welfare review.

First, Peter Lilley talked of initiating a constructive debate that was linked to the wish to focus social security on ensuring that people have the means to cope with modern life; to protect the vulnerable while safeguarding taxpayers' interests by controlling the size of the bill. No such debate, sadly, followed the publication of his two pioneering documents. The aim of a strategic welfare review must be to engage at each relevant point in the political and news cycles, and utilise this engagement to raise the fundamental questions that any such exercise will pose.

Second, a Delphic question was posed as to what the country should do when the social security budget looks set to grow significantly faster than national income. The postwar period had, until then, generally been characterised by the politics of the easy option. Increased benefits were paid, but their costs were met largely by the increase in revenue accruing to the government by rising personal incomes. That easy option is not now open to any government in the near future, not least due to trends in the labour market with which a strategic welfare review will need to reckon.

The Lilley review also managed, like the Phillips Committee had done, to identify those factors that had driven longer-term benefit expenditure upwards:

The factors driving benefit expenditure have been identified as demographic, economic, policy and social. The
following assumptions have been made for all the projections: no policy changes beyond those already in hand;
demographic changes in line with the Government Actuary's Department's population projections [...] The analysis shows that without a fall in unemployment, the social
security programme would continue to grow at around 3.3
per cent per annum. These projections allow for the fact
that there is very little growth projected in expenditure on
the elderly, as the number of pensioners will rise very little
before 1999/2000. This holds back expenditure growth
as spending on the elderly currently amounts to almost
half the total programme. In the early decades of the
next century the number of pensioners will increase significantly, putting substantial upward pressure on benefit
expenditure.[30]

Two comments are worth making here. Although unemployment has been reduced to a record low, there remain many
hundreds of thousands of people who have been consigned
to hopelessness in the ranks of the long-term unemployed.
Moreover, with the growth of the 'gig economy' and its
accompanying forms of casual and insecure work, the earnings of many of the people moving from unemployment into
work are not sizeable enough to pay much, if any, National

Insurance and tax contributions. Rather, despite the reining back of means-tested benefits for the low paid, large numbers of people on low income have to claim tax credits, housing benefit, or Universal Credit in order to make their poor wages up to a given acceptable standard of living. A falling number of people on unemployment benefit can no longer be equated, as it was in the Lilley days, with rising government expenditure as a result of the rise in the number of people in work.

Nevertheless, these papers were a noble one-off effort that we seek to incorporate in the regular strategic welfare review.

The most recent significant review of social security came when the coalition government sought to address the long-term economic and financial impact of its new state pension, through a provision in the Pensions Act of 2014. The act requires a periodic independent review to be carried out into factors affecting the future affordability of the state pension, such as the likely characteristics of the population and increases in the retirement age in decades to come. The review is also tasked with making recommendations on how the state pension edifice should be constructed to secure the welfare of older people over that period. This task fell for the first time, in 2016, to John Cridland of the Confederation of British Industry.

The resulting Cridland review, published in 2017, recommended both a fresh increase in the state pension age as well as the withdrawal of the Triple Lock, to help put the state pension on a more stable financial footing.[31] The review was able to forecast, under these recommendations, a reduction in state pension spending as a proportion of GDP by 2066–67.[32]

The May government initially accepted these two key recommendations, and the Prime Minister even went so far as to put a version of them to the country in her general election manifesto. Yet, as we outline later, one of them – the withdrawal of the Triple Lock – would later be buried underneath the rubble of the May government's collapsed majority.

It is that eventual rejection of the Cridland review's Triple Lock recommendation that opens up a broader challenge for any strategic welfare review.

Single reports on a particular part of the welfare budget are not seen as part of a total programme where many different groups begin to coalesce together to see that they have an interest in protecting and promoting the whole of a linked budget. Put another way, there is always a danger that a one-off review, presenting one set of needs that is not linked to others, will only have limited and partial appeal. Therefore, it is not enough for the government merely to invite a group of experts to submit first-class analysis on the longer-term outlook for a particular part of the welfare budget, and to put forward sound recommendations on the back of this analysis, if there is limited – or no – appetite for their implementation.

Clearly, in some areas of the welfare budget, voters wish to see expenditure increase. In other areas, they wish for it to decrease. Attempts at rebalancing the welfare budget to deliver a more equitable outcome – for example, between pensioners and non-pensioners – will be part of how the country defines and then works towards the common good after Brexit. What taxpayers have yet to be offered is a positive case for reshaping the whole of the welfare budget in this way, through which expenditure is clearly linked to outcomes that are deemed necessary in pursuit of that common good.

How might the government set about forging this new social contract with taxpayers? And what moves are required to ensure the social contract is upheld across and beyond the life of a single Parliament?

The goal of a strategic welfare review is to lock in a growing coalition of views behind an overarching strategy. Peter Taylor-Gooby highlights the opportunities that exist on this front, explaining how 'the newly important needs for child and elder care, education, training and opportunities, affordable rents, decent wages and more say in the workplace bridge across a range of social groups and rally a coalition of support for [a programme of increased expenditure]'.[33]

The pursuit of that goal in health and social care is the focus of the next chapter.

Back to Wanless?

There have been seven significant reviews of social care in the post-war period.

A 1957 report by the Royal Commission on the Law Relating to Mental Illness and Mental Deficiency was followed eleven years later by the report of the Committee on Local Authority and Allied Personal Social Services (the Seebohm Committee), which provided the social services delivery framework that would prevail for much of the post-war period.

A decade was to pass before the publication of *A Happier Old Age*, 'to develop a long-term strategy to ensure the wellbeing and dignity of all elderly people', and again before Gillian Wagner and Sir Roy Griffiths' reviews on residential and community care.

A Royal Commission was again the order of the day in 1997, tasked with exploring options for funding longer-term care that 'are fair and affordable for the individual and the taxpayer'. However, its key recommendations, such as the introduction of free personal care, were not acted on by the Blair government.

A similar fate was to await the most recent attempt at settling the financing of social care, made by the Dilnot Commission in 2011. The commission was established by the coalition government, under the chairmanship of Sir Andrew Dilnot, to review the funding system for social care in England. The commission's report, *Fairer Care Funding*, published in July 2011, found the current adult social care funding system in England to be confusing, unfair, unsustainable, and in need of urgent and lasting reform. It found likewise that people were unable either to plan ahead to meet their future care needs, or to protect themselves against high care costs. One of the report's key conclusions was that 'most people are realistic about the need for individuals to make some contribution to the costs of care in later life, but they want a fairer way of sharing costs and responsibility between the state and individuals and they want to be relieved of fear and worry'.[34]

Its central recommendation 'to protect people from extreme care costs' was to cap 'the lifetime contribution to adult social care costs that any individual needs to make at between £25,000 and £50,000. We think that £35,000 is an appropriate and fair figure.'[35]

Seven years have passed since then. There is no guarantee that, having been delayed time after time by the government – and diluted with each delay – this central recommendation will be implemented in any form, even by the end of this 'lost decade' for the welfare budget.

Perhaps partly out of frustration with the government's snail-like response to the central recommendation of the Dilnot Commission, and as a sign of the appetite that exists for a longer-term settlement covering major parts of the welfare budget, The King's Fund established its own commission in 2013, under the chairmanship of Dame Kate Barker, to look at the future financing of social care as well as the National Health Service (NHS).

The Barker Commission concluded that the consequences of 'doing nothing' would include fewer people receiving publicly funded social care, as further cuts to local authority budgets were forecast and more NHS organisations looked set to find themselves unable to provide timely access to acceptable standards of care within budget.[36] Under this scenario, people needing access to care would also have to continue to navigate the 'complexities and inconsistencies' of the fragmented systems of funding and entitlement. A similar stark picture was painted by the consumer group Which?. The organisation estimated in 2017 that within five years a shortfall of 42,000 beds would arise in care homes, leaving a quarter of elderly people in some areas unable to access the care they need.[37]

The Barker Commission went on to note that the costs of social care would fall increasingly on the shoulders of individuals and families, creating worry, uncertainty, and inequity on a scale that would be deemed unacceptable were it to apply in the NHS.[38] The commission listed a series of options: making critical care free as a first step would initially cost substantially less than £3 billion a year; making critical and substantial care free at the point of use for older people, as a second priority, would cost nearly £3 billion initially, rising to £14 billion by 2025 – an increase of £5 billion on existing trends; and meeting all levels of need, free at the point of use, would cost £7 billion initially and more than £20 billion by 2025 – some £11 billion more than on existing trends.

It then made the case for a mechanism to decide how much 'needs' to be spent in any given year on health and social care:

> [...] hand over the budget and the tax-raising powers to an independent body, for example, a new Office of Health and Social Care. It would be charged with assessing demand or need within the overall entitlements set by the government of the day, making a judgement on what efficiencies health and social care might reasonably be expected to achieve in any given year, and setting the budget, with the power to vary tax rates to keep the fund in balance.
>
> A weaker version would see an independent body make those assessments, offering transparent advice to the government of the day. That advice would cover spending levels, the balance of the tax against that, and any adjustments needed in the tax rate. The government would then accept or modify its recommendations.[39]

An independent body tasked with ensuring levels of service meet statutory obligations and public expectations, as well as informing the longer-term planning and financing of the service, was similarly a key recommendation resulting from the Competition and Markets Authority's study of the care homes market in 2017.[40]

As we record elsewhere in this volume, a House of Lords Select Committee recommended the use of such a mechanism in the NHS as well as in social care. Our recommendation is for an equivalent body to the NSC to take on this role for the whole of the welfare budget.

It was two House of Commons Select Committees – on Communities and Local Government, and Health and Social Care – that tried most recently to consider how a longer-term strategy might be applied to social care.

In 2017, the Communities and Local Government Select Committee set out the potential means of putting social care on a sustainable financial footing, as proposed by witnesses, including: a hypothecated tax through which a certain sized sum of monies raised from taxpayers would be set aside specifically to fund social care; restricting other areas of public expenditure on older people, by raising the age at which the state pension is set and ending the Triple Lock; and a mandatory social insurance mechanism, publicly owned and administered, and differentiated from voluntary private insurance mechanisms.[41]

Following that report, the Select Committee ran a joint inquiry with the Health and Social Care Select Committee.[42] The key function of that inquiry was to develop further some of the ideas that emerged in the previous year's work and, in doing so, to sketch out the beginnings of a longer-term funding framework.

The joint inquiry concluded that: the costings of future provision need to begin with a clear articulation of what good care looks like and what it costs; personal care should be delivered free to everyone who needs it; a new social insurance mechanism should be introduced and gradually extended to both health and social care; new forms of taxing wealth should be introduced to spread the burden of social care costs; and six principles should inform a longer-term strategy for social care (not to be confused with Beveridge's 'six principles' for postwar social security).[43]

In the reports that were published at the end of each inquiry, the Select Committees made clear that their aim was to influence the contents of a Green Paper on the financing of social care that had been promised, part of the way through the 2017 inquiry, by the May government. Although the Green Paper has yet to appear – more than a year after that promise was made – its publication is likely to signal the government's intention to apply a more strategic approach to the longer-term financing and provision of social care.

The Health and Social Secretary at the time, Jeremy Hunt, set out the 'seven principles' that will guide this approach.[44] However, to look in isolation at levels of funding and services within social care, without linking clearly with other aspects of the welfare budget, would represent a significant missed opportunity for the government as well as taxpayers. Besides, we have already shown that there is no guarantee of any such proposals relating only to one part of the welfare budget in this way being implemented. Hence the merit we attach to a proposal from Simon Stevens, the Chief Executive of NHS England, in respect of the support older people can expect to draw from the welfare budget.

He suggested in oral evidence to the House of Lords Select Committee on the Long-Term Sustainability of the NHS that:

> We need to go beyond just thinking about health and social care funding and think about what is happening in the benefits system, the pension system and so forth. Obviously, we have a Triple Lock until 2020, which is three different ways in which people's pensions go up. A new way of thinking about that would be a triple guarantee for old people in this country that would be a guarantee of income, housing and care. I do not think you can think about any one of those in isolation from the other two.[45]

This is the ethos that must guide regular strategic welfare reviews, if governments are to gain serious buy-in from taxpayers for the meaningful reform of social security, health, and social care.

Since the NHS was created in 1948, most one-off reviews

concerning it have focused on its internal organisation, rather than the longer-term costs associated with delivering specific health outcomes and how those costs are to be met.

One of the limitations that comes naturally to any longer-term funding reviews is that they are necessarily based on predictions and projections, such as demographic changes, as well as Rumsfeld's 'unknown unknowns'.

However, such limitations are far outweighed by the detrimental consequences of the absence of these reviews. One of those consequences, as noted by the Institute for Fiscal Studies (IFS) and the Health Foundation, has been that:

> Periods of feast tend to be followed by famine. The last two decades have been an extreme example of that. Planning for both feast and famine has been inadequate, and the consequences have been unnecessary costs, inefficiencies and uncertainty in the system.[46]

There have been just three significant post-war reviews concerning the NHS budget. The first was published seven years after the birth of the NHS. The Churchill government had commissioned an independent committee under the Cambridge economist Claude Guillebaud, to investigate the relationship between relatively high costs and the quality of the service patients could expect in return. Its conclusions were to rest, in part, on an economic analysis undertaken by Brian Abel-Smith, who had joined forces with Richard Titmuss and would go on to publish a book on the subject,[47] which found that a high-quality service was being delivered in an economical manner.[48] The committee also recommended that additional resources were required to support hospital modernisation and the extension of community care, but rejected the need for charges.[49]

According to Charles Webster, who was the official historian of the establishment and early years of the NHS, this was a disappointment to the Eden government. It had hoped to use the report to impose a regime of 'retrenchment' on the NHS. This is why, Webster suggests, 'no subsequent administration has dared to set up an independent inquiry into the cost of health care in the UK'.[50]

How might this political taboo be overcome? It is important to emphasise at this point that while a regular strategic welfare review would likely result in new demands on taxpayers' money, in return they would be given a clear statement of why additional expenditure is necessary and a clear set of objectives to measure the success of government policy. This would require the development of a new political culture, in which the government presents how it sees services, and the cash needed to provide them, developing over a set period of time. In reply, taxpayers would gain a greater understanding of, and have a part in accepting or rejecting those conclusions around, the financial demands that would be placed upon them to meet the improvements in welfare in the most general use of the term. This would go a long way towards addressing the paradox we set out at the very beginning of this volume.

The most recent major health review was published in 2013, when the NHS began its own high-profile attempt at gauging the longer-term financial challenges that would need to be overcome to protect basic service levels. Its first move was to publish a report setting out the most pressing challenges facing the service, 'including more people living longer with more complex conditions, increasing costs while funding remains flat and rising expectation of the quality of care'. The report, which was titled *The NHS belongs to the people: a call to action*, sought to open up a debate about the future shape of the NHS in order to treat rising numbers of patients, meet their expectations, and introduce new technology. It asserted that the combination of rising demands and NHS funding not rising above inflation could lead to a funding gap of £30 billion by 2020–21.

This exercise was completed by the NHS in the following year, with the publication of its *Five Year Forward View*. The document made plans to close the £30 billion funding gap 'by one third, one half, or all the way' depending on the combined efficiencies it could achieve and the funding options that would be pursued by the Treasury.[51]

Taken together, these two moves are indicative of the

skirmishes that have taken place since 2010 – the NHS has been battling relentlessly with the Treasury for the resources it deems necessary for survival.

As important as those skirmishes have been, in both squeezing additional upfront resources from the Treasury and finding room for greater efficiency, clearly they are no substitute for a framework that allocates resources based on a longer-term pattern of needs and expectations.

The closest thing we have had to such a framework, albeit on a one-off basis, rather than as part of an ongoing strategic welfare review, was offered up by a third major review – the Wanless review – which was established in part to help the Blair government fulfil its Budget commitment, announced in 2000, of a growth in health spending by 6.1 per cent for the period ending March 2004.[52]

Ed Balls, who was then Gordon Brown's Special Adviser at the Treasury, recalled how, at that time:

> We all came to understand in that Parliament that [an] incrementalist strategy in health was never going to work. We'd inherited a health service in which people were waiting up to eighteen months or more for hip operations or knee replacements. And those waiting times weren't going to come down unless we did something radical and raised the money to pay for it.[53]

Having settled on the need to do 'something radical', much effort was put into a broader strategy focused on:

> [...] working out how we'd get to that end point: make clear that the NHS needed more money; commission internal work to consider the tax options; launch an independent review into the future of the NHS; then steadily escalate the debate on the NHS so it would be the central issue at the next election, giving us a mandate to act afterwards.[54]

The task of conducting the independent review fell to Derek Wanless, the former chief executive of NatWest, whose interim report in 2001 assessed the likely funding requirements over the next twenty years.[55]

His final report, published in 2002, recommended that total health spending should rise in real terms by 7 per cent for the first ten years, and at a slightly slower rate for the following ten years, thereby increasing from 7.7 per cent of GDP in 2002–03 to between 9.4 per cent and 9.5 per cent in 2007–08, between 10.3 per cent and 11 per cent in 2012–13, between 10.6 per cent and 11.9 per cent in 2017–18, and between 10.6 per cent and 12.5 per cent in 2022–23.[56]

Here is where the final part of the Balls strategy was put into place. As he was formalising the government's acceptance of the Wanless recommendations in his Budget statement, Gordon Brown announced that they would be funded by increases in National Insurance contributions for both employers and employees, and that further reform within the NHS would be expected in return for this major increase in funding.

Although he was convinced in the lead-up to this announcement that it would lose Labour the next election, Mr Brown's 2002 Budget was the most popular one he ever delivered during his decade at the Treasury.

We believe there are two lessons to draw from that moment of triumph, both of which should help to steer a strategic welfare review.

First, the source of revenue (i.e. how we pay for increased funding) is crucial to the success of any meaningful reform. As Ed Balls noted, 'It was the symbolism of National Insurance that made the difference: the feeling that you pay in when you're working to ensure that when you lose your job, when you need the NHS, when you retire, you're going to be protected and looked after.'[57] This marked a clean break from much of the post-war period, in which increased expenditure on health was, in effect, paid for by cutting expenditure elsewhere.[58]

Second was the Wanless methodology itself, based on defining what a high-quality health service in 2022 should look like, and then determining what additional resources would be required to deliver it, given a range of potential variables both in the demand for healthcare and in the cost of supplying it.

Rather helpfully, again when thinking about the structure of a strategic welfare review, Wanless identified a number of factors, both in demand and supply, which would affect how much it would cost for the services to become a reality. On the demand side, he identified: changes in age structure within the population, while noting that demographic change is not the main factor driving up healthcare costs; changes in the health status of the population, both in terms of its general health and the extent to which increased life expectancy results in extra years of good or ill health; and changes in the likelihood of people seeking healthcare for a given level of need.

On the supply side, he identified: the rate of spending on technology, both in terms of medical advances and use of IT; changes in pay and productivity of NHS staff; and the wider productivity of the NHS.

It is in the Wanless report that we see a pristine model of analysis and implementation that is ready to be applied to the welfare budget as a whole. However, if it is to have a lasting effect on the government's programme to secure the welfare of the population, rather than secure a one-off increase in revenue for a particular service, this model will need to be applied regularly through a strategic welfare review.

As a further lesson for today's politicians, a crucial part of Wanless' vision was for 'no bottlenecks between health and social care, with patients moving from hospital as soon as they are medically fit to do so, and a choice of residential or nursing home placement for patients who cannot be cared for appropriately at home'. In the absence of a strategic welfare review, that part of the vision will remain elusive for all too many patients.

Later, in 2006, Wanless published an additional document with The King's Fund, independent from the government, on the likely cost of social care in two decades' time, and the funding arrangements required to ensure the money is available and 'supports high-quality outcomes'. In so doing, he posed a series of questions that could apply to the whole of the welfare budget, and the answers to which would lie in the conduct of regular strategic reviews:

> At the heart of the issue should be a debate about what social care will do in the future. How will it help people? What outcomes should it aim to achieve? Who should it help?
>
> [Despite considerable sums spent on social care] there is little information about whether this spending achieves the government's desired aims for older people of promoting choice, independence and prevention.
>
> There is also widespread dissatisfaction with the current funding system. In part this results from ignorance about what to expect. It often comes as an unwelcome surprise to older people to discover that social care is means-tested and they are expected to rely on their own savings and income

until their assets have fallen to the threshold set for state-funded care. It is a common complaint that the existing system penalises those who have saved for their old age.[59]

Clearly such thinking helped to shape the work of a House of Lords Select Committee – set up in 2016 specifically to examine the long-term sustainability of the NHS – which reached similar conclusions to those we reported earlier from the IFS and Health Foundation, in that:

A culture of short-termism seems to prevail in the NHS and adult social care. The short-sightedness of successive governments is reflected in a Department of Health that is unable or unwilling to think beyond the next few years. The Department of Health, over a number of years, has failed in this regard. Almost everyone involved in the health service and social care system seems to be absorbed by the day-to-day struggles, leaving the future to 'take care of itself'[...]

Funding for health and adult social care over the past 25 years has been too volatile and poorly co-ordinated between the two systems, and this should be addressed as a matter of priority. We recommend that the budgetary responsibility for adult social care at a national level should be transferred to the Department of Health which should be renamed the 'Department of Health and Care' [...]

We are concerned by the absence of any comprehensive national long-term strategy to secure the appropriately skilled, well-trained and committed workforce that the health and care system will need over the next 10–15 years. In our view this represents the biggest internal threat to the sustainability of the NHS. Health Education England has been unable to deliver. It needs to be substantially strengthened and transformed into a new single, integrated strategic workforce planning body for health and social care which should always look ten years ahead, on a rolling basis [...]

Our conclusion could not be clearer. Is the NHS and adult social care system sustainable? Yes, it is. Is it sustainable as it is today? No, it is not. Things need to change.[60]

In line with the themes we identified earlier in this volume around the NSC, as well as one of the Barker Commission's key recommendations, the Select Committee proposed the establishment of an Office for Health and Care Sustainability. This new unit would be tasked with looking fifteen to twenty years ahead, and reporting to Parliament on: the monitoring and publication of authoritative data relating to changing demographic trends, disease profiles, and the expected pace of change relating to future service demand; the workforce and skills mix implications of these changes; and the stability of health and adult social care funding allocations relative to that demand, including the alignment between health and adult social care funding.

The Select Committee recommended also that the current government and any successive governments should agree financial settlements for an entire Parliament to improve planning and ensure the effective use of resources, while 'shadow' ten year allocations should also be agreed for certain expenditures, such as medical training or significant capital investment programmes that require longer-term planning horizons.

Since then, the Prime Minister has announced plans for a significant increase in the NHS budget over a five-year period. We look later in this volume at how a strategic welfare review could help the government build on, and finance, that commitment.

With a handful of notable exceptions, one-off reviews tend to have had little long-term effect on the pursuit of our national welfare. Each of these reviews has involved much work and made a series of serious recommendations, although all too many have been characterised by crises in a particular budget, an overriding desire to cut costs in a particular budget, and a failure to see through key recommendations for changing policy.

Even where the Wanless review has had a big effect on the size of taxpayers' contributions to the NHS, this has been eroded over time as costs, and the age of NHS patients, have changed so that the original answers given in 2002 have been undermined. Likewise, where the Turner Commission has had a big impact on the future of retirement incomes, by paving the way for flat-rate universal pensions set above the level of means tests, the government has had to legislate for further similar reviews – without necessarily implementing their recommendations – in an attempt to meet the accompanying costs. Nor has the government addressed in the round – so as to include income, care, and housing – the key issue of providing for old age.

This again makes the case for a strategic welfare review that is run on an ongoing basis and which would regularly remind taxpayers and the government that to merely stand still in policy, even for a short while, can result in hard-earned advances being undermined.

Later in this volume, we will bring together what we think the overall objectives of a strategic welfare review should be, that is, what outcomes we believe taxpayers' revenue should support in respect of social expenditure.

The shortcomings in policy that are associated with the absence of such a review have been touched upon in this chapter. We look next at how the lack of such objectives that are clearly defined and generally accepted by the electorate has allowed the government since 2010 to make major changes to the living standards of some groups of people relative to others and take no account of the unprecedented transfer of wealth that occurred by the policy of quantitative easing.

A dangerous vacuum

In this chapter we look mainly at the outcomes of the coalition government, in the absence of an agreed broader strategy for the welfare state, partially achieving its objective of reducing the mega budget deficit it inherited. For those who believe that the welfare budget was bloated and ready for major cuts, the lack of a strategic welfare review allowed this objective to be achieved without undue public scrutiny. Those who, whatever their views about the size of the welfare budget, believe that any changes should ensure that the poor are protected, went into battle without an overall picture of what individual cuts amounted to.

It is the size of the welfare budget that has ensured it is always at the front of the queue when politicians are seeking to rein in public expenditure. This has never been truer than when the coalition government came to attempt to reduce public borrowing and close the budget deficit.

In June 2010, the Chancellor of the Exchequer, George Osborne, spent a significant portion of his emergency budget statement following the formation of the coalition government addressing 'the largest bill in government – the welfare bill'. The crux of his argument was that 'it is simply not possible to deal with a budget deficit of [over £150 billion] without undertaking lasting reform of welfare'.[61]

The Chancellor expanded on this point in his spending review statement six months later, adding:

> We have chosen to cut the waste and reform the welfare system that our country can no longer afford. [...] As I said in June, the more we could save on welfare costs, the more we could continue other, more productive areas of government spending. [...] I have announced real reductions in waste and reforms to welfare, and although that will reshape public services to meet the challenges of this time, I think it is the right choice.[62]

Although he concentrated his attention on social security, other parts of what we will call for to be included in a strategic welfare review also suffered major funding difficulties. It is true, nevertheless, that the most severe cuts fell on social security.

As a result, there have been downward trends since 2010 in every part of the welfare budget – in real terms, as a proportion of GDP, and as a percentage of overall public expenditure, with the exception of health. Even this point of exception requires clarification.

Despite the health budget being more heavily favoured than other areas of public expenditure, and taking a bigger chunk of national income since 2010, over the past eight years health spending has grown more slowly than in any comparable period since the NHS was founded.[63] Moreover, the health budget of course faces its own unique inflationary pressures, such as the cost of new drugs and equipment, above and beyond retail and consumer prices.

The decision to reduce the size of the overall welfare budget in order to radically reduce the deficit resulted in a reduction in net public borrowing of over £100 billion: from £153 billion (9.9 per cent of GDP) in 2010 to £45.2 billion (2.2 per cent) in 2018.[64] At the same time, successive chancellors have cut company taxation and raised the personal allowance, in an attempt to reduce the tax burden on businesses and the low paid.[65]

Running counter to the arguments made in favour of constraining the welfare budget and easing some of the financial burden on taxpayers who finance it are the longer-term consequences for society that arise when, in real terms, the state succeeds in cutting whole swathes of the welfare state.

How many families, particularly the poorest, must go without a suitable home, an adequate care package, a good school place, timely hospital treatment, or even a hot meal each day, if the government decides on behalf of taxpayers it has not consulted that it cannot, or will not, meet the necessary costs?

Among the side effects of the deficit reduction strategy pursued since 2010 has been an increase in primary school class sizes (following a decade of decline until 2011). Secondary school class sizes, likewise, reached their highest level in more than a decade in 2017 – no surprise, therefore, that the attainment gap between the average student and white working-class boys has remained stubbornly wide. There were 11,000 fewer beds available in NHS wards in 2016–17 than in 2010–11. 27,000 more households were living in temporary accommodation in 2017 than in 2010; over the same period the number of rough sleepers in England grew from 1,768 to 4,751 (although research from Crisis puts this latter figure at 8,000, with a further 8,000 seeking refuge in tents and cars, or on buses and trains).[66] In 2016, an estimated 1.2 million older people were not receiving the social care they needed – an increase of 48 per cent since 2010.

Looking ahead, the IFS estimates that the tax and benefit reforms announced since 2015 will reduce the poorest households' income by 11 per cent. Heavy losses of at least 5 per cent will be sustained by households across the poorest third of the population. The richest third, meanwhile, will be better off as a result of the changes.[67]

Stark inequalities have also revealed themselves in families' ability to access a GP. The total number of GPs serving patients within the bottom (most deprived) quintile of the population, in which ill health occurs more frequently, fell by 1,166 between 2010 and 2017, to 7,696. The total fell for the second quintile by 750, to 7,767; for the third quintile by 532, to 7,230; and for the fourth quintile by 233, to 6,163. Meanwhile, in the top (least deprived) quintile, the total increased by 5, to 4,192. The tale of woe does not end here.

Looking more broadly at the difficulties emerging in the NHS since 2010, Lord Darzi found that: inequality in life expectancy is severe and getting worse; there are particularly acute health inequalities for the most disadvantaged groups; there is a new epidemic of loneliness; there has been a deterioration in access to urgent and emergency care; there have been significant delays in non-urgent and planned care (in March 2018, around a quarter of patients had been waiting longer than eighteen weeks for treatment); access and timeliness in primary and community care has been deteriorating; compared with other countries, access to new and innovative treatment is poor and getting worse; the progress made on vaccinations and immunisations is beginning to reverse; and the gap between the hours of social care needed and received by people on the lowest incomes has reached 23 per cent, as against 14 per cent in the middle and 8 per cent at the top.[68]

As troubling as these findings are, the reader could be forgiven for expecting even worse outputs and outcomes, given that public spending on adult social care fell by 10 per cent between 2009–10 and 2016–17, with similar trends found also in levels of expenditure on primary care.[69] Much of the reason that so many patients continue to be treated so well, of course, is the dedication and ingenuity of so many front-line nurses, doctors, and care workers.

In his examination of welfare in America, Robert Myers
sought to grapple with a more fundamental issue, evident in
the following observations, around longer-term shifts in the
size and functions of the welfare budget:

> Should social insurance provide only a basic floor of pro-
> tection upon which individuals and, in part, their employ-
> ers should build, with public assistance for the small
> minority whose basic needs are still not provided for? [...]
>
> Or should the Government supply complete economic
> security to the aged, disabled, and the survivors of deceased
> workers so as to replace virtually the full wage loss? [...]
>
> What then are the implications in other areas, such as
> medical care for the total population? [...]
>
> If all persons should be guaranteed the highest possible
> quality of medical care by the Government, should there
> also be guarantees that none should have incomes substan-
> tially below the average, or that all should have diets of the
> highest nutritional quality, regardless of whether they can
> afford, and wish, to do otherwise?
>
> There is a basic, important question to be decided on
> the future role of social insurance in a country. There is a
> choice to be made, and all the facts on both sides should
> be presented to the citizens, so that they can make wise
> decisions.[70]

That exercise has yet to be undertaken in this country. Rather, we have seen a totally different turn of events unfold in piecemeal fashion over the past decade, with no consideration of the overall impact of public expenditure changes on our national welfare. Here are two consequences of such an approach.

First, as expenditure has risen in one part of the welfare budget, it has been compensated, directly or indirectly, by cutbacks in other parts. Pensioners' incomes have been protected, for example, while successive waves of benefit cuts have been imposed upon vulnerable single people of working age and families with children. According to the IFS, in the early days of the Cameron government in 2015, pensioners had been helped into a position in which they had higher incomes on average than the rest of the population, once housing costs and family composition were taken into account.[71]

Average incomes from pensioner benefits rose by a total of 2.1 per cent in real terms between 2011–12 and 2014–15, compared with a real-terms cut of 7.5 per cent in benefits paid to working-age families.[72] Likewise, pensioner poverty was, by 2016, 6.2 percentage points lower than a decade earlier, compared with 2.1 percentage points lower for children and 1.1 percentage points higher for working-age non-parents. The IFS also recorded that pensioners now have the lowest absolute poverty rates of all the major social groups.[73]

Overall, real-terms spending on tax credits fell under the

coalition government, from £31.7 billion to £30.6 billion, as did spending on Child Benefit, from £13.4 billion to £11.9 billion – although the number of children increased by 200,000, from 13.2 million to 13.4 million. The real-terms education budget, meanwhile, fell from £100.6 billion to £87.5 billion, as did housing from £36.1 billion to £33 billion.[74]

As a proportion of public expenditure, the overall welfare budget increased from 76.8 per cent to 77.6 per cent. That overall increase, accounted for by health, disguised falls of 0.1 percentage points in tax credits, 0.2 percentage points in Child Benefit, 1.6 percentage points in education, and 0.4 percentage points in housing. Meanwhile, as a proportion of GDP, the welfare budget fell from 34 per cent in 2010 to 31.4 per cent in 2015.

What is the longer-term fiscal redistribution resulting from this short-term political choice? The House of Commons Library forecasts that social security expenditure in cash terms, encompassing the Department for Work and Pensions and HM Revenue & Customs (HMRC), will increase from £207.5 billion in 2012–13, to £241.1 billion in 2022–23 – an increase of £33.6 billion. Of that overall cash increase, £26.6 billion (79 per cent) is accounted for by pensioners.

The picture appears very different if cash demands are expressed in real terms, or as a proportion of GDP. In real terms, the overall social security budget will fall in that decade, from £223.8 billion in 2012–13 to £222.3 billion in 2022–23. Yet pensioners will have seen a real-terms increase of £7.3 billion over this period of time. All of the cuts therefore will have been borne by the working-age population – a fall of £8.8 billion – and this is an outcome that no post-war government has ever before set out to achieve.

Drilling even deeper into the data, the Children's Commissioner has forecast a real-terms cut of 17 per cent in social security spending, per child, between 2009–10 and 2019–20. Alongside this is a real-terms cut of 20 per cent in spending on children's services.[75]

Among the outcomes of these cuts has been a widening of the gap in household income between families with children above and below the poverty line. Jonathan Bradshaw and Antonia Keung have found that, in 2007–08, the median poverty gap before housing costs was £41.60 per week, but by 2016–17 it had increased to £57.40 per week. After housing costs the increase was from £50.40 per week in 2007–08 to £63.00 per week in 2016–17.[76]

A second consequence of proceeding without a strategic welfare review is that cutbacks or shortcomings in one part of the welfare budget can trigger sizeable expenditure in another. The real-terms cuts in local authorities' expenditure on social care, for example, from £15.84 billion in 2010–11 to £14.91 billion in 2016–17 have resulted in increased pressures on the NHS budget. The National Audit Office estimates that the gross annual cost to the NHS of keeping in hospital older patients who no longer need to receive acute clinical care – just one consequence of those cuts – is in the region of £820 million.[77] As another example, the annual cost to the NHS of poor housing is estimated to be £1.4 billion,[78] while we have estimated that the cost to health and social care services of malnutrition and hunger among the elderly – often arising as a result of inadequate social care packages – will reach £13 billion in 2020, rising again to £15.7 billion by 2030.[79]

Causative links exist, too, between changes in the labour market and the growth of the welfare budget. Snapshot data reveal that a 10 per cent increase in involuntary unemployment in a given area lowers life expectancy by a year.[80] Similarly, in explaining persistently low life expectancy (and with it the strain of ill health on public services) in certain parts of the country over an extended period of time, The King's Fund revealed that, holding other factors constant, a 5 per cent increase in involuntary unemployment – a visible sign of failure in the welfare budget, as well as wider economic policy – increases fivefold the chances of an area having persistently low life expectancy.

This chimes with the longstanding research, dating back to Dennis Marsden's findings in 1975, demonstrating that as their length of unemployment increased, unemployed men's physical health deteriorated and they lost a sense of meaning in their lives as well as their sense of identity. Likewise, in 1994 Duncan Gallie and Carolyn Vogler found that 'the unemployed had notably poorer physical health scores than people in employment', and were more likely than other social groups to rely frequently on GPs and hospital services. In sum, and picking up on the health of those workers trapped in insecure jobs and on very low pay, in a state of involuntary precariousness, 'labour market experience was closely connected with the level of dependence on collective welfare provision. Those in more disadvantaged labour market positions had poorer psychological and physical health and made more frequent use of local health services.'[81]

The causative link between longer-term unemployment and poor health was most recently highlighted by Sir Michael Marmot. In his 2010 review of health inequalities, commissioned by the coalition government, Marmot identified 'steady negative effects, proportional to the duration of unemployment, which progressively damage health [...] adverse effects on health are greatest among those who experience long-term unemployment'.[82]

He went on to identify three key ways in which unemployment affects levels of morbidity and mortality. First, financial problems as a consequence of unemployment result in lower living standards, which may in turn reduce social integration and lower self-esteem.

Second, unemployment can trigger distress, anxiety, and depression. Many psychological stressors contribute to poor health not only among the unemployed themselves, but also among their partners and children. Loss of work results in the loss of a core role which is linked with one's sense of identity, as well as the loss of rewards, social participation, and support.

Third, unemployment impacts on health behaviours, being associated with increased smoking and alcohol consumption and decreased physical exercise.[83] Professor Marmot concluded that 'the longer a person is unemployed, the risk of subsequent illness increases greatly, and thereby further reduces the likelihood of returning to employment'.[84]

These longstanding findings remain troubling because, as we mention elsewhere, despite record low levels of headline unemployment, there remain several hundreds of thousands of people among the ranks of the long-term unemployed – in September 2018, there were 562,000 people in this country who had been unemployed for six months or longer.[85] Many of them live in communities that have been rocked by the economic headwinds of globalisation. To give an idea of the social groups within which this misery is likely to be concentrated, a separate piece of research we commissioned from the House of Commons Library shows that over the past two decades, employment rates among men with a degree have increased from 80 per cent to 90 per cent; with GCE/A-levels have remained at 80 per cent; with GCSEs have fallen from 78 per cent to 75 per cent; and with no qualifications have fallen from 58 per cent to 52 per cent.

Moreover, many of those who have moved into work in

recent years have found themselves in low-paid jobs of poor quality, which are at least as detrimental to their physical and mental health as unemployment. Broader shifts towards out-sourcing and casualisation of low-skilled jobs, combined with the growth of the 'gig economy', mean there are now nearly 4 million people working on insecure zero-hours contracts, in low-paid self-employment, or as agency workers. In 2017, just over a million workers said they were working part-time because they could not find a full-time job – an increase of 51 per cent over a decade.

Not surprisingly, in the light of these longer-term shifts in the labour market, the working class have become increasingly likely since the turn of the century to describe themselves as being in 'not good health', while other social groups towards the top of the ladder have moved in the opposite direction. In the decade leading up to 2011, among people in:

- routine occupations, the increase in the proportion of people describing themselves as being in 'not good health' was 3.5 percentage points, from 8.3 per cent to 11.8 per cent;
- semi-routine occupations, the increase was 1.8 percentage points, from 6.9 per cent to 8.7 per cent;
- lower supervisory and technical occupations, the increase was 1.9 percentage points, from 6.5 per cent to 8.4 per cent;

- intermediate occupations, the increase was 0.6 percentage points, from 4.8 per cent to 5.4 per cent;
- lower managerial, administrative, and professional occupations, there was a decrease of 0.3 percentage points, from 4.5 per cent to 4.2 per cent; and
- higher managerial, administrative, and professional occupations, there was a decrease of 0.5 percentage points, from 3.2 per cent to 2.7 per cent.

Yet no meaningful attempt has been made at gauging the impact of these trends on the health budget, or indeed reversing them. With this in mind, how might a strategic welfare review seek to extend and improve the quality of people's lives, while easing some of the pressure on certain areas of the welfare budget, through a sustained increase in the numbers of decent jobs in those communities that feel, often justifiably, as though they have been left to rot by globalisation? We return to this question later in the volume, with a proposal for one way in which a strategic welfare review could counter such trends in the labour market.

The ongoing tug of war, between those who advocate in favour of the piecemeal enlargement of the welfare budget and others who instead favour its retrenchment, has come to dominate much of the political agenda since the Second World War. Much of this tug of war has taken place in the absence of a fully thought-out strategy for the welfare budget as a whole, tied to specific objectives for securing our national welfare.

And so we find ourselves marooned in our present situation where, as described even by the World Economic Forum, 'severely underfunded state social systems are at breaking point, employers are backing away from traditional employment models and social protection contributions, and individuals once again are shouldering a larger share of the risks'. The forum further noted that 'new systems will need to address gaps in social protection across typical life events including periods of education, raising families, work including career gaps, retirement, and later elder care'.[86] For short, in the absence of an ongoing strategic welfare review, more and more of life's risks are being unloaded onto the shoulders of individuals, no matter how vulnerable they are or what ability they have to bear those risks without collective support.

Taking a thirty-year view of such developments, Tony Atkinson commented that 'in considering the future it is easy to become depressed. In part such depression is rife because we have lost sight of the objectives we are trying to pursue.'[87] He also outlined the options for what a strategic welfare review could entail, in seeking to counter these developments: first, the restatement of ambitions to provide a set of yardsticks; second, a clear narrative as to how the ambitions could be fulfilled; and, lastly, the execution of a coherent set of policies to so fulfil them.[88] It is this rallying cry of Atkinson that drives us forward to consider how best we can more rationally marshal our resources while being quite transparent on what the objectives of expenditure are. Too many poorer people have been failed in the absence of a strategic welfare review that tries to look at a total vision of welfare expenditure as it relates to the wellbeing of our society, within which a care for the poor should have a priority.

The absence of any serious work along these lines, and the accompanying absence of any major objectives, has long bedevilled the welfare budget, and will continue to wreck the lives of current and future generations who end up having to bear disproportionately large risks at different stages of their lives. As Nick Timmins set out in the closing pages of his history of the post-war welfare state, there has been an 'ongoing problem of how to measure success. It is easy to measure 'inputs' – for example more money. But what does that buy? Usually more 'outputs' – more staff, more equipment, better buildings, more programmes, for example. But does that in turn produce better 'outcomes'?'[89]

It would be equally true to say that while Timmins was concerned partially with how one measures success, we are now in a position where it becomes more relevant to measure failure. It is the failure side of the overall welfare budget that we have picked up in this chapter, and with which we close it by outlining some of the human consequences of the developments we have covered.

Neither the current government nor any of its predecessors has pursued anything like a coherent strategy for the size, allocation, and desired outcomes of the welfare budget. The results of the major changes to the welfare budget since 2010 have been characterised by largely undebated major shifts in the distribution of welfare expenditure. We are left guessing at the real-terms impact such monumental shifts have had on health and social care services, for example, as well as the overall living standards of the poor. Likewise, no overall consideration has been given as to how the failure to maintain the historic real-terms rise in NHS expenditure has fallen on other budgets, and vice versa. We analyse in the following chapter how the political dynamics behind Brexit and the 2017 general election lend themselves to the creation of a strategic welfare review along such lines.

What the lack of a strategic welfare review means to individual families

It is not too difficult to spot a broader pattern of cuts in the welfare budget that have brutal side effects. We refer here to the backlogs in a stretched NHS – bad enough in themselves – and the scuppering of vulnerable families' eligibility for social security benefits, as well as appropriate housing and schooling. We have several examples, including the recent plight of families in Birkenhead, which reveal the human face of this broader pattern.

The first family had to wait a year for an appointment with a paediatrician. Throughout this year, the child struggled at school and was excluded on several occasions. They could not be transferred to a more appropriate setting until after the appointment. In the meantime, they had to endure a wasted year of schooling.

A similarly placed family were seeking to determine their eligibility for child disability benefits and a more suitable home, as one child suffers with a severe form of autism that, as well as restricting their own life chances, has wreaked havoc on the wellbeing of their sibling with whom they share a bedroom. During their eight-month wait for a paediatrician's appointment, the family's benefit claim was rejected as they were unable to present a paediatrician's report. Nor could they successfully apply for a house which would enable each sibling to have a separate room.

We find a third example at the other end of the scale. A woman from Birkenhead recently found herself amongst an army of women born in the 1950s whose state pension age was raised by successive governments, without adequate notice being given for her to rearrange her plans for retirement. She is having to continue working as hard as she always has done to make ends meet, even though the physical demands of having spent decades in a manual workplace are taking a huge toll. In fact, her ankles have become so worn that she is currently unable to work.

While the increase in the state pension age, in one part of the welfare budget, made it vital for her to remain in work, cutbacks in another part have diminished the women's ability to do so. She was due recently to undergo an operation on her ankles, but this has been postponed (again) due to the constrained resources in the NHS. The woman is therefore out of work and trying to survive on a very low income, in a great deal of pain.

In another recent case in Birkenhead, a mother and her five children had to sleep in one room because each of their other bedrooms was plastered with mould. The children's breathing had suffered because of the mould. The property was described as 'a deathtrap' due to the hazardous state of the electrics, and neither the heating system nor the cooker had been fixed by the landlord. A second mother reported similarly that her children's breathing began to suffer, after her calls and messages to the landlord about severe damp went unanswered for six months.

Meanwhile, a working man recently sought help from one of Birkenhead's food banks. Like all families without money he, his partner, and their two children were hungry. Destitution hangs like the sword of Damocles over the head of those families suffering a double whammy of benefit cuts. The first cut inflicted upon this family involved a mega reduction in their Universal Credit payments. The second was a steep drop in Personal Independence Payments.

During the same week in which the family sought help from the food bank, the two children had to be kept out of school for two days because they didn't have any money to buy lunch and did not qualify for free school meals. So much for social mobility.

Political necessities

The government is, not surprisingly, devoting an enormous amount of energy to the task of negotiating the UK's new role in the world after Brexit. With the enormity of that task in mind, and considering also the political tightrope along which the government must walk following the wipeout of its majority at the last general election, it would be tempting to conclude that any prospect of a clear strategy to guide the size, allocation, financing, and objectives of the welfare budget will be parked in a political vacuum forever and a day. The country must not allow this to happen.

The path for which we instead advocate is built on the assumption that the dynamics that brought about Brexit lend themselves to a major reform of the welfare budget, which demands nothing less than a radical transformation of our country. The decisive votes that carried the referendum in favour of Leave were cast by mainly working-class voters, who felt that their families – and in some cases their entire communities – had become quietly disenfranchised under successive governments.

The central argument advanced here is that, as our country opens up a new chapter in its history by leaving the EU, a task of almost equal importance to negotiating our new role in the world is to initiate a revolutionary programme of domestic reform. The driving force behind that programme should come from a strategic welfare review which, while seeking to boost the country's overall standard of living, focuses relentlessly on protecting those groups who have been put at a severe disadvantage by longer-term social and economic upheaval. The backdrop to this argument comes from an analysis of the EU referendum result that was undertaken by Matthew Goodwin and Oliver Heath.[90]

Goodwin and Heath found that people living in the poorest households were much more likely to support leaving the EU than those in the wealthiest households. In households with incomes of less than £20,000 per year the average support for Leave was 58 per cent. In households with incomes over £60,000 per year support for leaving the EU was only 35 per cent. Those out of work were also far more likely to support Brexit than those in full employment – support for Leave among the former was 59 per cent, but only 45 per cent among the latter. Meanwhile, people engaged in low-skilled and more manual occupations were much more likely to support leaving the EU than those working in more secure professional occupations – on average the Leave vote among the former was 71 per cent but among the latter was only 41 per cent.

What, if anything, does this tell us about the role of a reformed welfare budget in post-Brexit Britain? First, given the importance of place, community, and country to those who voted Leave, there must be a renewed role for the welfare budget in defining our national borders, through access to certain benefits and services, for example, and training the necessary numbers of people to fill vacancies in frontline services such as social care.

Second, a renewed focus is required on a particular area of policy – the Foundation Years – which is absolutely fundamental to the life chances of children from poorer and working-class backgrounds and for which there is currently no coherent strategy.

Of the sixty-five parts of the country where children born into less affluent homes tend to have the fewest opportunities for social mobility, sixty gave politicians a smack on the nose by voting in support of Brexit. More than two thirds of voters in Great Yarmouth, Mansfield, Doncaster, Barnsley, Walsall, Dudley, Tamworth, and Blackpool – identified by the Social Mobility Commission as being among our worst 'cold spots' – voted Leave. Similarly, in Barrow-in-Furness, where only 38 per cent of children achieve a 'good level of development' by the age of five, 61 per cent of voters opted for Leave. Similar figures were to be found in Allerdale, West Somerset, Newark and Sherwood, and Ashfield, to name just a few areas.

Not surprisingly, given their starting position, younger people born into poorer or working-class homes in many parts of the country tend to leave school with fewer skills and qualifications than their more fortunate peers. Alongside structural changes in the labour market, these forms of disadvantage make it much more difficult for younger people growing up against these backgrounds to find and keep a decent job in later life. Partly as a result, and again in combination with structural changes in the housing market, they are less likely to have access to a decent home, or to lead a long and healthy existence.

Herein lies the potential for a strategic welfare review, which responds to and counters such realities in neighbourhoods up and down the country, to form the cornerstone of a post-Brexit renaissance which restores millions of families' stake in society, by helping them to succeed in life through a system that mitigates alienation and embodies the fact that the population is looking after its own. This must be a starting point in the negotiation of a new social contract. It must also begin from the perspective of equalising children's life chances in those first crucial years of life before they start school.

It would have been nigh on impossible for the government to conduct a strategic welfare review prior to Brexit, while we had open borders. How can any politician seek to plan, with a straight face, a long-term education budget if he or she has no idea how many families will move freely from the EU and settle here, for example? Assuming that the implementation of border controls and balanced migration becomes government policy post-Brexit, this will enable us to plan on a firmer footing when it comes to the size and composition of the population.

A strategic welfare review in post-Brexit Britain could give the government the political space it needs to lead an honest national debate on the long-term costs of, and desired outcomes from, the welfare budget – both in securing our national welfare and combatting the 'diswelfare' triggered by injustices in the labour and housing markets. That way, by the time the country next goes to the polls, the government will have demonstrated to voters its understanding that there is much more to life, and its own record, than Brexit. Brexit will instead have served as a launch pad for a mega programme of social reform.

The EU referendum, followed a year later by a general election, has given the political kaleidoscope an almighty shake. A total recasting of the welfare budget in favour of those whose living standards have been left to decay in recent times, is the single biggest task that voters have set their politicians on the domestic front.

An argument along these lines was deployed by some of the key members of the Prime Minister's campaign team, in the run-up to the 2017 general election and on the back of the speech she had given on the steps of Downing Street on the first day of her premiership:

> If you're from an ordinary working-class family, life is much harder than many people in Westminster realise. You have a job but you don't always have job security. You

have your own home, but you worry about paying a mortgage. You can just about manage but you worry about the
cost of living and getting your kids into a good school.

If you're one of those families, if you're just managing, I
want to address you directly.

I know you're working around the clock, I know you're
doing your best, and I know that sometimes life can be a
struggle. The government I lead will be driven not by the
interests of the privileged few, but by yours.[91]

Their goal was to base the Prime Minister's electoral appeal
on plans for a programme of social reform capable of addressing many of the dynamics behind the Brexit vote. This strategy
could have been a sound one, had it not been undermined by
the contents of the programme itself.

The case put forward by the Prime Minister in the run-up to
polling day in June 2017, bearing the hallmarks of the Cridland
and Dilnot reviews, maintained that our population in the
coming decades will be older and more of us will live longer;
as such, many more people will draw upon the pensions and
social care services that help us sustain a relatively healthy and
independent existence for as long as possible in later life; and a
major challenge stems from the inadequate financing of social
care – more of us will spend greater periods of time in hospital beds that, as a result, cannot be used to treat people below
retirement age who require emergency care or routine surgery.

Moreover, the state pension age will need to keep rising if the costs of meeting commitments not only to maintain but also to increase the value of the state pension against earnings and inflation are to be met.

May's manifesto promised that if the Conservative Party were returned to government, it would: replace the Triple Lock on the state pension with a Double Lock; introduce a means test for Winter Fuel Payments; align the future basis for means testing for domiciliary care with that for residential care, by taking into account the value of the family home along with other assets and income, whether care is provided at home or in a residential or nursing care home; introduce a single capital floor, set at £100,000, rather than the current means-tested limit of £23,500, so that people would retain at least £100,000 of their savings and assets, including value in the family home; and extend the current freedom to defer payments for residential care to those receiving care at home, so no one would have to sell their home in their lifetime to pay for care.

The Prime Minister sought to base her campaign on the assumption that, by identifying and then being seen to face down these longer-term challenges to our national welfare, she possessed the unique qualities of strength and decisiveness required to safeguard the wellbeing of the population. The electorate, though, was far from convinced. How so?

Voters took the Prime Minister to task for failing to deal with these challenges in a way that chimed with their own sense of justice and fair play. This most basic of tests for reformers was spelled out by Sidney Webb in a 1919 Fabian tract on the financing of public expenditure, where he cautioned that 'it is vital to our character that nothing should be done that would outrage, not justice, as to which there is no abstract definition of validity, but the sense of justice of the community'.[92]

The tidal wave of voter hostility to the manifesto proposals, particularly around social care, exposed the government's failure to give anywhere near enough thought to how a new social contract should be forged with the public, both as beneficiaries of and financial contributors to the welfare budget. The government was unable to explain how many pensioners would lose their Winter Fuel Payment, for example, or to justify how people with conditions such as dementia could end up bearing a disproportionately heavy burden to finance their social care.

Voters made clear that they would not accept the terms being offered by the Prime Minister. That refusal was rooted not in any kind of hostility towards an increase in expenditure on social care services – although perhaps a great deal more effort could have been put into articulating why such an increase was needed – but rather over the question of whether the Tories were offering the fairest and most sustainable means of financing that increase.

Hence the spectacle in the days that followed the publication of the manifesto, of the Prime Minister trying to scramble together an altogether different proposal for an 'absolute limit' on how much people would have to pay towards their social care. This proposal, said the Prime Minister, would feature among a whole series of ideas to be consulted upon in a Green Paper. By this time, though, the self-inflicted damage was irreparable.

The government sailed needlessly into the choppiest of political waters during the general election – as Lord Darzi put it, 'the 2017 general election put social care on the political map, even if all for the wrong reasons'.[93] It did so by trying to navigate the financing of social care through the lens of how individuals should bear the risk of meeting the costs of their own care, from their own assets. What the election proved is that even the sturdiest looking vessels can capsize when they come into contact with voters' resistance to politicians' sticky fingers dangling over the home they wish for their loved ones to inherit. Lessons will need to be applied quickly if the government is to avoid a similarly stormy situation further down the line, when the time comes again for it to try reshaping the welfare budget.

One lesson we draw from the general election is that the government must move from a debate on how it can offload more financial risks onto individual citizens and their families to one in which it enables us collectively to pool our risks through a reinvigorated National Insurance system. Crucial to the functioning of this system, and in building support for it, is the ability to keep politicians' sticky fingers away from people's assets.

Likewise, to ensure adequate financial contributions are raised in as just a way as possible, it must be based on a progressive system of National Insurance contributions. As Brian Rodgers noted:

> [National Insurance] is a tax which is less unpopular than most, for it is based, both in theory and in popular thinking, on the concept that the recipient of benefit is entitled to that benefit as a right. It is this element in social insurance that is its greatest strength, and which justifies the maintenance of the insurance function, for it has possibly done more to maintain and strengthen the sense of human dignity in times of tragic distress than any other social service.[94]

Had a strategic welfare review been functional prior to the general election, it might well have steered the Prime Minister away from the social-care-shaped trap that ensnared her parliamentary majority, not least because she might just have gauged from voters the level of service and outcomes they expected from the welfare budget, and how they wished to meet the costs of delivering them.

If voters are to be presented with a seriously thought-through set of options ahead of the next general election, and a rerun of the 2017 campaign is to be avoided, the Prime

Minister will need a strategic welfare review to produce answers to eight fundamental questions about our future:

- What will be the key characteristics of our population in ten years' time?
- What are the most pressing challenges, over the next ten years, to the quality of life of different groups in the population, and particularly the most vulnerable?
- On current trends, and under the present funding mechanisms, which of those challenges are likely to prove the most difficult for the welfare budget to meet?
- How effectively are the needs of the population being met by the current distribution of the welfare budget?
- Which reforms, if any, are required to help us most effectively meet the needs of the population over the next ten, and even twenty, years?
- How much will it cost to devise and see these reforms through, to meet those needs?
- What is the fairest and most sustainable way of raising the money needed to meet those costs?
- What outcomes need to be measured, to reassure taxpayers that their money is being used as effectively as possible?

The Cabinet would then be able to work backwards from the answers to those questions, in devising a series of reforms and the means of financing them.

The Prime Minister has at least begun to try, albeit rather hastily in the heat of a general election campaign, to initiate a public debate on the future of the welfare budget. This attempt took the form of questioning how much expenditure should be directed towards the pensioner population, and who should foot the bills for that expenditure.

To some extent, her attempt was successful – rarely has social care featured so heavily in the run-up to a general election. But what the Prime Minister failed to envisage was that the lion's share of this debate would take place on the adverse consequences of her manifesto proposals.

Having barely seen the light of day during the general election, any semblance of a long-term strategy for the welfare budget, and with it the prospect of a reallocation of resources to meet the needs of our society over the next generation, is fast disappearing into the thick political fog.

This is not due solely to the social care debacle. The flagship proposals in the manifesto to curtail the cost of pensioner benefits were also ditched as part of the Prime Minister's confidence-and-supply agreement with Northern Ireland's Democratic Unionist Party. This concession will contribute to the long-term enlargement of the welfare budget, with as of yet no clear means of paying for these additional sums.

Our plea to the government is to rescue a long-term strategy from the thick political fog. A first piece of equipment for that rescue mission already exists and is there to be grasped.

The Office for Budget
Responsibility – a key player

Two of the issues we seek to address in this volume are what role a strategic welfare review can take on in gearing public policy towards meeting the needs of the population in years to come, and how it can apply the lessons from defence, an area of policy that has been the subject of a dozen strategic reviews since the Second World War.

The creation in 2010 by the Chancellor of the Exchequer, George Osborne, of the Office for Budget Responsibility (OBR) could be seen as a game changer on this front. Building up a regular strategic welfare review will be a mega task. However, as we show in this chapter, the OBR has proved itself to be more than capable of pulling together most of the nuts and bolts required to do so. It is the political appetite to unleash those capabilities that remains lacking.

Here we explore what role a beefed-up OBR could play in welding together the different priorities and policies for each part of the overall welfare budget, and giving them a longer-term outlook, as part of a strategic welfare review.

The OBR was set up to 'address past weaknesses in the credibility of economic and fiscal forecasting and, consequently, fiscal policy', by examining and reporting on the sustainability of public finances, with a remit of investigating 'the impact of trends and policies on the public finances from a multitude of angles, including through forecasting longer-term projections and balance sheet analysis'.[95] It has fulfilled that task by publishing its economic and fiscal outlook alongside each Budget and Autumn statement, as well as an annual fiscal sustainability report and forecast evaluation report.

The immediate impact of the OBR's publications was to introduce an unprecedented level of credibility to the longer-term economic and fiscal projections that were delivered by the Chancellor to the House of Commons.

In 2013, sensing how successful this innovation had been, Osborne asked the OBR to take on two additional responsibilities: to assess the government's performance against a nominal cap on social security expenditure and, in order to facilitate an open debate on the matter, to 'prepare and publish information on the trends in and drivers of welfare spending within the cap'.

Here is an example of how politicians can best set up and use independent bodies to prepare the public for decisions that they wish to take. Osborne in this instance wished to enact further cuts to the rate of growth in welfare expenditure. Knowing the hostility that this would gain, he sought coverage by adding to the OBR's tasks the one of preparing the ground for such an assault.

Within the first few years of its life, therefore, the OBR

has been given the task of setting out detailed long-term fiscal projections, as well as those social and economic factors that are likely to push up, or drive down, expenditure on social security. It has quietly, and unspectacularly, begun to bring together the data we need for a strategic welfare review:

- In its first report on trends in social security expenditure, published in 2014, the OBR presented a broad survey of historical trends alongside its judgements on the prospects for benefits and tax credits spending.
- Its second considered the UK's public spending on social protection – a broader definition of welfare spending – in the international context.
- The third report looked at how policy changes affected welfare spending over the 2010–2015 and the then-planned 2015–2020 Parliaments, relative to a counterfactual in which spending increased in line with demographics and pre-existing uprating policy.
- The most recent instalment centred upon the likely impact of the government's flagship welfare reform, Universal Credit, on total expenditure.

This work, which more recently has also encompassed long-term pressures on health expenditure, lays the basis for a strategic welfare review.

A central recommendation we make here is for the OBR's regular examination of the welfare state to stretch beyond social security, to encompass health and social care, then as a second step to education and housing. And clearly it will need strong backing and impetus from the Prime Minister, otherwise stacks of useful analyses risk being neglected and underutilised.

The terms of reference set for the OBR will be crucial. For health and social care, the Prime Minister will require projections to take into account a number of variables – what will happen to the level of demand, for example, under different scenarios for population growth, in different care settings, under different eligibility criteria, by different sizes of workforce, with the impact of different types of treatment, and so on? Likewise, what set of variables could be pieced together into a coherent strategy, based on different methods of paying for its implementation?

Looking at the welfare budget as a whole, and with the OBR's projections seen as the foundation upon which to do so, we would argue that a strategic welfare review should then begin to develop its work along the following lines:

- What should be the minimum adequate level of service delivered through each component of the welfare budget?
- What are the costs associated with these levels?

- How will those costs change in the years ahead?
- What are the options for meeting those costs?

The OBR has, in effect, been girding its loins for this task by quietly pulling together the tools that politicians will need to devise a strategy for the welfare budget.

In its 2016 report on welfare trends, for example, the OBR noted that a likely increase in social security spending between 2015–16 and 2020–21 of 6.5 per cent in cash terms would mean that spending is set to fall by 2.3 per cent in real terms and by 1.4 per cent of GDP.[96] The report states further that by 2020–21, it will have fallen as a share of GDP for an unprecedented eight consecutive years. The overall drop, of 2.1 per cent of GDP since 2010–11, would be the biggest on record across two consecutive Parliaments, similar in size to that seen during the late-1980s economic boom.

But the cause of the drop in social security expenditure as a proportion of GDP couldn't be more different. In the earlier period, a period of rapid economic advance, with national income rising fast, government expenditure naturally fell as a proportion of GDP. In contrast, in the more recent period, which has been characterised by less dynamic growth, the opposite is occurring for the very simple reason that the government has set out deliberately to cut the amount of benefits being paid to families with children. It is the combination of these two factors that accounts for the overall fall against

GDP of social security expenditure. The present policy would take welfare spending back to roughly the share of GDP it occupied prior to the financial crisis of 2008. But while social security spending in support of pensioners would also have fallen to around its pre-crisis level, spending in support of children and working-age people would be at its lowest level of GDP since 1990–91.[97]

Likewise, in 2017, the OBR analysed the longer-term effects on the public finances of an ageing population and further upward pressure on health spending from factors such as technological advancements and the rising prevalence of chronic health conditions.

Its analysis found that, with no change in policy over the next fifty years, the state would end up having to spend much more as a share of GDP on age-related items such as pensions, and in particular health, but with no additional revenue. Its warning could hardly have been more stark: 'In the absence of offsetting tax rises or spending cuts this would widen budget deficits over time and put public sector net debt on an unsustainable upward trajectory.'[98] In other words, a big increase in expenditure directed towards older people will need to be offset by an equal decline in other areas.

The OBR found that the main drivers are upward pressures on key items of welfare spending. Even under the current models, without factoring in any potential improvements in the standards of each service:[99]

- Health spending rises from 6.9 per cent of GDP in 2021–22 to 7.6 per cent in 2026–67, 9.1 per cent in 2036–37, and 12.6 per cent in 2066–67 – a total increase of £111 billion in today's terms.
- State pension costs increase from 5 per cent of GDP in 2021–22 to 5.3 per cent in 2026–27, 6.2 per cent in 2036–37, and 7.1 per cent in 2066–67 – a total increase of £40 billion in today's terms.
- Long-term social care costs rise from 1.1 per cent of GDP in 2021–22 to 1.3 per cent in 2026–27, 1.6 per cent in 2036–37, and 2 per cent in 2066–67 – a total increase of £17.5 billion in today's terms.

That this increase in long-term social care costs is so modest helps to demonstrate just how limited the existing services are. This is partly why we advocate for a strategic welfare review to look at improved standards, which will increase this proportion of expenditure to GDP. But even then this would hardly come close to the increase forecast by the OBR for health and state pension costs.

Meanwhile, expenditure on working-age social security benefits is forecast to remain relatively constant at 4.3–4.5 per cent of GDP.

The upshot is that, setting aside interest and dividends and including no improvements in the levels of services, spending on the ageing population as a proportion of all public expenditure will increase steadily from 55 per cent in 2016–17 and 2021–22 to 56 per cent in 2026–27, 59 per cent in 2036–37, 60 per cent in 2046–47, 62 per cent in 2056–57, and 63 per cent in 2066–67.[100]

Similarly, as a proportion of GDP, spending arising from our ageing population will increase from 19.8 per cent in 2021–22 to 21 per cent in 2026–27, 23.4 per cent in 2036–37, 24.6 per cent in 2046–47, 26.1 per cent in 2056–57, and 27.7 per cent in 2066–67.

On current policy, overall public expenditure, minus interest payments, will increase as a proportion of GDP from 35.8 per cent in 2021–22 to 37 per cent in 2026–27, 39.3 per cent in 2036–37, 40.6 per cent in 2046–47, 42.3 per cent in 2056–57, and 43.8 per cent in 2066–67. Yet the tax take will stay constant at 36–37 per cent of GDP over the next fifty years, meaning the government will either have to borrow more or make further cuts to the level of service provision.[101]

In a sign of how formidable that task will be, successive governments have run deficits in all but fourteen years since 1948. Annual public expenditure has averaged at 39.8 per cent of GDP while annual revenues have come in at 37.4 per cent. The last time annual revenue exceeded 37 per cent of GDP was 32 years ago, in 1986.

This should strike terror into the hearts of politicians. Put more politely by the OBR:

The main lesson of our analysis is that future governments are likely to have to undertake some additional fiscal tightening beyond the current consolidation planned for the next five years in order to address the fiscal costs of an ageing population and upward pressures on health spending.[102]

The cost of raising taxation to 43.8 per cent of GDP over the next half a century, to cover the costs of public expenditure in 2066–67 and so as not to incur additional borrowing, is £117 billion in today's terms – equivalent to a £0.25 increase in the basic rate of income tax – even without improving public services. That is not a misprint.

Again this must be the starting point of any negotiations between politicians and taxpayers who, without a significant shift in opinion, could be facing the prospect of a return to the welfare state of the 1930s.

We certainly hope the OBR will continue to undertake the kind of analysis that it presents annually and to make it comprehensive in a way that, with our limited resources, we cannot. But even if the OBR did continue to produce more comprehensive data, its political weakness would become ever more obvious. It is not owned by anybody, least of all the Cabinet as a collective decision-making unit.

No strategic defence review would have worked if an independent body at arm's length from government undertook the bulk of the work. It would have been all too easy for them to be ignored. Likewise with the OBR, which, we believe, should be tasked with reporting to an equivalent body to the NSC: its data need to be central to the work of any such decision-making body – and to Parliament.

We turn in the next chapter to a second key ingredient of a strategic welfare review: what the public is likely to expect from different services and what it is willing to pay for. It is on the basis of those expectations that politicians will need to respond with a package of proposals for their fulfilment, how they are to be funded, and how their outcomes are to be measured. Again, history hands us a helpful precedent with which to shape this exercise.

What does the country want from the welfare budget?

At the time when Britain claimed it was standing alone during the earlier years of the Second World War, governments still had the confidence to set in hand not only the great war histories of how British society responded to total war, but also to begin setting out what the public believed should be the basis of a new society. The task of finding out what the public thought was given initially to the Ministry of Information. A similar exercise should begin today and should be carried out regularly as part of a strategic welfare review.

In November 1942, the Ministry of Information produced a paper that had been prepared by the Home Intelligence Division titled *Public Feeling on Post-War Reconstruction*. The paper was requested by the Paymaster General, to gauge public feeling on the nature, extent, and source of demands for reconstruction plans, as well as any specific points strongly felt by the public as desirable in such plans.

The paper detected the general mood of the country as being 'a mixture of hopes, expectations and fears. Hopes are greater than expectations, and fears are greater than hopes.'

Running through all hopes for the future were six key objectives:

- there must be work at a living wage for everyone who is capable of doing it;
- private profit must cease to be the major incentive to work – everyone must work primarily for the good of the community;
- there must be financial security for everyone who is unable to work;
- there must be decent homes for everyone at a cost which will not reduce people to poverty;
- the same education must be available to everyone so that all will have an equal chance; and
- in the future, the best possible medical, surgical, and hospital treatment should be available to everyone, 'without the stigma of charity'.

It was on page eight of the document that the key objective of a post-war welfare budget was set: 'Three years ago, the term social security was almost unknown to the public as a whole. It now appears to be generally accepted as an urgent post-war need. It is commonly defined as "a decent minimum standard of living for all".'

The reforms put forward for the achievement of this objective for the welfare budget were:

- work for all who are physically and mentally able to work, with a standard minimum wage based on the cost of living;

- family allowances to parents, both in order to
  encourage an increase in the birth rate, and to
  enable parents to prolong their children's education;
- adequate pensions 'above the poverty line' for
  widows and orphans;
- adequate unemployment allowances, 'without the
  taint of charity' – though it is hoped that these will
  seldom be needed;
- adequate sickness allowances, so that financial
  anxiety shall not be added to the inevitable worry
  that ill health brings; and
- adequate and earlier old-age pensions for all.

Likewise, on the means of financing a post-war welfare
budget:

- 'The level of war expenditure has led the great
  majority to believe that finance cannot, in future, be
  regarded as a barrier to achieving [social security],
  and "even if it involves the continuation of high
  taxation, it is well worth the price".'
- 'The general view is that the cost of these proposals
  is such that no contributory scheme could meet
  them, even though "higher contributions would
  cheerfully be paid".'
- 'Graded contribution, based on earnings or income,
  would be willingly accepted.'

- 'The continuance of anything in the nature of a
  means test is generally condemned. It is felt that
  no poor person should be "penalised for thrift".
  Measures penalising thrift among the wealthy are,
  however, less widely resented.'

We have now a not-dissimilar survey to that of the wartime
Ministry of Information, although it is much more scientifi-
cally based. It is undertaken by the National Centre for Social
Research (NatCen), in its British Social Attitudes survey. The
latest report records that, for the first time since the financial
crash of 2007–8, more people (48 per cent) want taxation
increased to allow greater public spending than want tax and
spend levels to stay as they are (44 per cent). However, while
these figures represent notable changes as compared with
recent years, they still only represent a partial move back to an
earlier mood. The 48 per cent of people who now want more
taxation and spending is in contrast to the joint-record low of
32 per cent in 2010, and highs of 63 per cent in 1998 and 65 per
cent in 1991.

These surveys in public opinion will form a significant
contribution to the work of an equivalent body to the NSC
as it seeks continually to gauge the objectives taxpayers have
in mind for the welfare budget, as part of its task of driving
the strategic welfare review. A recent NatCen report also
recorded that people's top priority for more spending remains

as it has always been – health. Around eight in ten people think the government should spend more or much more on health (83 per cent). Moreover, the report showed that, for the first time in more than thirty years, pensions are not the public's top priority for extra spending on benefits. The proportion identifying retirement pensions as being among their top two priorities for extra welfare spending is now 60 per cent, down from 72 per cent in 2014 and the lowest it has ever been. It seems that the public have recognised the fact that successive governments have been successful in raising the relative incomes of pensioners and this may be an area where people are beginning to feel increased spending is no longer needed.[103]

How might these conclusions help to shape a strategic welfare review?

First, if voters do decide that an expansion of the welfare budget is necessary, to meet the costs of establishing a world-class health and social care system, for example, the strategic welfare review would be required to present costs to help shape the public debate on tax changes, if they were required, and if the belief was that the economy could sustain such a level within the growth of GDP. Politicians will need to take care to keep that expansion within the limits of what taxpayers feel they can afford and the economy can sustain.

Second, a crucial part of this strategy will involve the development of methods of financing the welfare budget that are felt to be fair and bearable – what balance should be struck between general taxation and National Insurance contributions, as well as between public and private provision? – while also considering what limits need to be applied to the expansion of the welfare budget, without putting at risk the services upon which particularly vulnerable groups rely.

Third, as the costs go up – and taxpayers are asked to foot this (growing) bill – so might the resistance to meeting them, particularly if the quality of service is deemed not to have risen commensurate with its growing budget. Hence the need in those circumstances, if budgets do rise, of introducing new governance arrangements that record how those monies are being spent and what outcomes are attached to them.

Fourth, taxpayers seem willing to accept that taxing the wealth of the rich alone will never build up a sufficient war chest for the welfare budget. Additional contributions will be required from all of us. But taxpayers will naturally ask first whether resources could be reallocated from one part of the welfare budget to another, or raised from the most fortunate households first, before any additional sums are requested from the broader population.

Again this brings us back to the fundamental question of what forces pose the greatest risk to our quality of life, and how the welfare budget should be organised and financed to counter those forces. Moreover, who should be entitled to services, how do we wish those services to differ from today, and do we wish for the welfare budget to be more, or less active than it is now?

Perhaps one clue is to be found within a British Social Attitudes survey released in April 2018 by The King's Fund, showing that:

- There was a growing consensus that the NHS is facing a funding crisis. Out of all respondents to the 2017 survey, 86 per cent agreed that the service faces a major or severe funding problem – an increase of 14 percentage points since 2014.
- 61 per cent of respondents supported tax rises to increase NHS funding, up 21 percentage points from 2014.
- 35 per cent supported a separate tax that would go directly to the NHS, while 26 per cent would be happy to pay more through their existing taxes.
- A majority of respondents supported tax increases to pay for the NHS across all age and income groups, including 61 per cent of the highest earners.
- In 2017, 56 per cent of Conservative Party supporters backed a tax rise to pay for the NHS, up from 33 per cent in 2014. Support among Labour Party supporters stood at 68 per cent in 2017, up from 53 per cent in 2014.[104]

A second clue comes from a ComRes poll conducted in January 2018, which found that four in five adults would support a penny increase in National Insurance contributions if this money were ring-fenced to fund only the NHS.[105]

In addition, a recent Demos survey registered that:

> Not one participant in our focus groups expressed the sense that the NHS is currently performing well, and we observed lengthy observations about a decline in standards and the poor treatment of staff [...] there was a clear understanding of the social care crisis and the impact this is having on the core health service. Participants again referred strongly to the need for a contributory system, and many stated that they had "paid in" their share over the course of their lives.[106]

Looking more broadly at the welfare budget, and in another example of the post-Brexit politics that could help to shape it, NatCen found that 62 per cent of voters on lower incomes believe that the government should guarantee a job to everybody who needs one.[107]

The outlines of an agreed position from taxpayers, on the terms of their social contract with the state, are becoming clearer. Taxpayers favour approaches to the financing and delivery of the welfare budget that centre upon contribution and shared responsibility. If indeed the country can unite around a small grouping of priorities for the welfare budget – combining individual initiative and self-improvement with state support that pools collective risk and aims to meet specific needs – and the OBR is able to provide the data on how those priorities can be achieved (and paid for), how might politicians move to meet these demands?

A social contract for post-Brexit Britain

Brexit necessitates a new contract between Britain and the world. It must also be seized as an opportunity to produce a new social contract between taxpayers and the state.

The first strategic welfare review, conducted by an equivalent body to the NSC with support from the OBR, will help the Cabinet to draft this first post-Brexit social contract. Each subsequent review will then enable successive governments to renew the contract and reshape services accordingly.

What services should each citizen expect to receive from the welfare budget, and what duty does the state have to ensure they are received? Moreover, what duties should the state expect of each citizen in return, either financially or behaviourally? And what reforms are required both within and separate from the welfare budget, to reduce current and future cost pressures?

The strategic welfare review will have a role of updating and presenting coherently what the OBR has produced already, extending the OBR's terms of reference to cover all aspects of the welfare budget as we have defined it, opening up the debate on what taxpayers want from the welfare budget, estimating the costs of meeting taxpayers' expectations, and proposing bold means of meeting them.

A process of negotiations centring upon the current state of the welfare budget, its ability to cope with future demands, how it can be better interrelated and spent to achieve the overall goal of the common good, and the costs of enabling it to do so, will lay the groundwork for a strategy that governs its constituent parts. It will also equip politicians and taxpayers with the information they need to determine overall satisfaction with the welfare budget, and the levels of finance that taxpayers are willing to provide, through certain governance arrangements, to sustain its operation.

An equivalent body to the NSC will, on the basis of the lessons gained from earlier chapters, play a central role in that process by conducting regular strategic welfare reviews in which it collates the necessary data through the OBR; uses those data to report on the longer-term trends in different needs that affect living standards, the cost of providing services and benefits to meet those needs, and the options for meeting those costs; carries out extensive public engagement as part of its task of setting objectives for the welfare budget, as well as building awareness of and support for those objectives and their delivery; and ensures that the objectives that have been set are delivered.

We make a first attempt here to set four overall objectives for the welfare budget, to propel us towards a post-Brexit vision of the common good that guarantees, as a first step, national minimum levels of service, income, and thereby outcomes.

The three principles upon which those four objectives are built are the importance of shared contributions towards the common good, investment in children's life chances, and prevention of social evils – including the 'diswelfare' generated by the labour and housing markets – which could hurt any one of us, but are disproportionately likely to afflict the poorest. As Peter Taylor-Gooby writes, these principles 'reframe the issues to stress common identities and aspirations between low-income and more comfortable people rather than pointing specifically at redistribution to the poor'.[108]

In pulling these principles into a strategy for the welfare budget, we draw upon the headings of Beatrice and Sidney Webb's blueprint, published in 1913, for what would eventually become the welfare state, in pursuit of 'a definite standard minimum of the conditions of civilised life, below which, in the interests of the whole, no individual shall be permitted to fall'.[109] The Webbs defined the 'national minimum' as consisting of 'sufficient nourishment and training when young, a living wage when able-bodied, treatment when sick, and a modest but secure livelihood when disabled or aged'.[110]

In a sign of the influence the Webbs exerted upon the early stages of his career, as well as the influence we are about to show that both they and he have had on the shaping of our proposed objectives, Winston Churchill developed this line of thought in a speech to St. Andrew's Hall in Glasgow, in 1906. He told his audience that:

I am of the opinion that the State should increasingly assume the position of the reserve employer of labour [...] the State must increasingly and earnestly concern itself with the care of the sick and the aged, and, above all, of the children. [...] I look forward to the universal establishment of minimum standards of life and labour, and their progressive elevation as the increasing energies of production may permit. [...] We do not want to pull down the structures of science and civilisation: but to spread a net over the abyss.[111]

The idea of the state marshalling a proportion of taxpayers' money, as well as its legislative power, to establish 'minimum standards of life and labour' held firm in Liberal thinking, as well as in Fabian socialism, in the early twentieth century. In 1918, for example, Herbert Henry Asquith set out how:

I should be prepared to adopt for myself and to recommend to my friends as a convenient and appropriate watchword and summary the formula of a National Minimum. In concrete terms, I understand that to mean that we ought not to be content, until every British citizen, man, woman, and child, has in possession or within reach a standard of existence, physical, intellectual, moral, social, which makes life worth living, and not only does not block but opens the road to its best and highest possibilities [...]

The same idea of a National Minimum ought to inspire and direct the inevitable and much-needed reconstruction of the relations between capital and labour [...]

There is no task on which the State could more fruit-fully expend its thought and energy than the prevention of unemployment, which means the discouragement of slack work, and, what is perhaps still more important, the banishment from the lives of the workers of the spectre of insecurity [...].[112]

On the Fabian side, G.D.H. Cole developed the idea of the national minimum along the following lines:

Society ought to afford all its members, irrespective of their virtues or vices, their strength or weakness, a toler-able basic standard of living, high enough to keep them in health and reasonable comfort and to enable them to bring up their children after a fashion that will allow them, in their turn, as far as possible, an equal chance of making the best of their lives.[113]

Beveridge, meanwhile, stated that his review of social security:

[...] as a whole is intended to give effect to what I regard as a peculiarly British idea: the idea of a national minimum.

My Plan for Social Security is part of a policy of a national minimum. The idea of a minimum wage [...] is necessary but isn't sufficient. There is wanted also a minimum income for subsistence when wages fail for any reason; a minimum of provision for children; a minimum of health, of housing, of education. A minimum needn't be static; in every field it should progress. But being a minimum only leaves it room and incentive to individuals to add to it for themselves according to their personal capacities and desires. The national minimum – preserving the maximum of liberty and room for progress while putting an end to want and other evils – is a peculiarly British idea. My Report is intended to give effect to that idea in one important field – that of income.[114]

This policy of the national minimum was described by Sidney Webb as being the 'necessary basis of society', and we believe it must underpin a post-Brexit strategy for securing our national welfare. As a second move, this strategy must also look at opening up opportunities for social mobility to all children and young people, regardless of their backgrounds.

With the mind's eye fixed firmly on the dynamics that triggered the Brexit earthquake, we propose four objectives, outlined in the following sections, as a starting point for these negotiations.

Objective 1: The Prevention of Unemployment

A stronger safety net will guard against destitution while simultaneously helping to lift the country towards genuine full employment, without compromising on minimum labour standards.

The government is committed to the achievement of full employment. Yet the size of the welfare-to-work budget for the long-term unemployed has been slashed, and there remains a hard core of more than half a million men and women among their ranks.

The dynamics of Brexit necessitate a fresh public examination of the details of this evil – its causes and consequences – thereby priming the country for a fresh assault, bringing jobs and the possibility of a higher quality of life to those parts of the country that have become accustomed to lacking both. Even though headline rates of unemployment are among the lowest they have ever been in this country, the jobless rate in September 2018 stood at 9.5 per cent in Hartlepool, 8.3 per cent in Newcastle, 7.6 per cent in Bootle, 7.3 per cent in Middlesbrough, 7.2 per cent in Grimsby, and 7.1 per cent in Birkenhead, for example. Similarly, the employment prospects of lower-skilled males have suffered hugely over the past two decades – the employment rate among those with no qualifications fell from 58 per cent in 1996 to 52 per cent in 2016. To carry on ignoring this malaise would be to ignore the social ills that helped tip the EU referendum in favour of Leave.

We propose a job creation programme, which begins with the state guaranteeing six months' paid work in either the private, non-profit, or public sector for people who have been unemployed for six months or longer. A major attraction is that those enrolled on the programme would maintain good habits, make new connections, and contribute to the improvement of their local community while earning a living wage to spend in that community. They would also have increased their attractiveness to other potential employers by being on the scheme rather than continuing to languish on benefits. Tax-payers, meanwhile, would see the advantages of their monies being spent not on benefits, but on jobs that deliver visible improvements to the quality of life in their communities.

According to the House of Commons Library, the cost of abolishing long-term unemployment in this way among young people would be in the region of £500 million. The cost of doing so for every adult who is long-term unemployed – around half a million people – would be in the region of £3 billion. Hence the idea of rolling out the programme in stages, rather than with one big hit.

A further task on this front, to guarantee a minimum level of income and security, is for the Department for Business, Energy and Industrial Strategy to establish and rigorously enforce minimum standards to protect the whole of the working population – guarding against low-paid bogus self-employment and the abuse of agency or zero-hours labour, for example – to relieve some of the pressures exerted on the NHS by workers' poor physical and mental health, as well as the pressure exerted by their low earnings on the social security budget, while simultaneously increasing tax revenues. The need for urgent action on this front is demonstrated by the plight of 700,000 people working in the 'gig economy' for less than the National Living Wage. Companies plunge their workers below the minimum by falsely labelling them 'self-employed' while continuing to exercise almost total control over them.

Meanwhile, negotiations between taxpayers and the government will need to determine the levels at which benefits are set – and how they are administered – to ensure they cover more adequately the cost of living among families with children, single households, childless couples, and disabled people as well as pensioners, without being deemed unaffordable or excessive.

As a supplementary measure, if the state is to provide ladders of opportunity in the labour market, a revamped skills programme will need to link apprenticeship training – particularly in those sectors most sensitive to the prospect of labour shortages, such as construction – to a post-Brexit border system of immigration controls. This will also help to accelerate the speed at which new houses can be built.

Finally, the government could open a totally new front in welfare reform by creating a network of local employment services for all low-paid workers (going beyond the current service for Universal Credit claimants). This reform would represent a next stage in the life of Jobcentre Plus that gives families a realistic chance of climbing away from the bottom of the labour market. Ideally those services would have a relatively broad reach among the low-paid, to bring together work opportunities and help workers take advantage of those opportunities. Its main benefit would be the provision by a dedicated caseworker of information, advice, and guidance, as part of a clear and agreed contract aimed at helping workers earn more money and, crucially, overcoming the barriers that currently prevent them from being able to do so.

The expertise of the OBR would be vital in forecasting future levels of long-term unemployment, as well as its spatial distribution, the scale rates required in each year to guarantee an adequate minimum standard of living, and the projected costs and savings associated with each of the policies proposed in pursuit of this objective.

Objective 2: A National Minimum of Child Nurture

The country shall ensure that every child, regardless of their background, starts school on a level playing field.

The politics of Brexit also lead us to look at the need for a new Foundation Years contract to revolutionise the life chances of children born into poorer or working-class families.

Around half of the inequality that exists in children's

readiness for school, between those from relatively wealthy homes and others from poorer homes, is accounted for by what happens at home, mainly in respect of the style of parenting and the home learning environment.[115] Overall, the impact on children's life chances of what happens at home balances fairly evenly by the age of three with the impact of childcare and early education.[116] Research published by the Department for Education suggests that, further:

> The effects of [the] home environment and demographic factors upon child development outcomes at age four years were often substantially greater in size than the effects of [early education and childcare]. These findings highlight the important role the home environment can play in child cognitive and socio-emotional development, particularly warmth or invasiveness in the parent–child relationship, and the Home Learning Environment. This suggests potential benefits of approaches to support parenting and the Home Learning Environment.[117]

While mega sums of money have been invested by successive governments in early education and childcare, the country has yet to demand the investment of equivalent sums in services that focus on parenting and the home. That is despite the 'strong evidence' found by Sir Michael Marmot 'that early intervention through intensive home visiting programmes during and after pregnancy can be effective in improving the health, wellbeing and self-sufficiency of low-income, young first-time parents and their children', in particular, and that:

> [...] sensitive and responsive parent–child relationships are associated with stronger cognitive skills in young children and enhanced social competence and work skills later in school. It is therefore important that we create the conditions to enable parents to develop this relationship during the child's critical first year.[118]

Pioneering new interventions that seek to improve maternal mental health, strengthen the bonds between parent and child, and create a home environment that enables babies and infants to develop, are being piloted but only on a relatively small scale. The weight of evidence shows that such interventions hold the key to equalising children's life chances during those crucial first years of life which all but determine whether or not they will grow up to become poor adults.

One example is the potential for an intensive home visiting programme, which seeks to improve children's early cognitive and social development. The programme would work with parents with very young children, through twice-weekly home visits of thirty minutes each over an eighteen-month period, to help them prepare their children for school. Each child would also be given a free high-quality book or educational toy each week and the trained visitors would not only help the parents bond with their child – in a similar way to the Home Start model – but also equip them with the skills and confidence they need to support their child's learning at home. The estimated cost of delivering a programme along these lines is between £2,800 and £5,000 per child, depending on the mix of volunteers and staff. If the programme had been made available to all 600,000 poorer babies and infants in 2015–16, a quarter of their age group, its cost would have been between £1.6 billion and £3 billion.

Clearly the negotiations here will centre upon the number of children being born over the next decade, as well as the intensity of the programme and the mix between paid and voluntary staff. We see the OBR's role here being to forecast the numbers of children likely to be eligible for the programme in each of the next ten years, and to adjust cost forecasts based on different ways of administering the programme.

Alongside this programme, it would be worth considering proposals for frontloading children's benefits so that, at nil extra cost to the taxpayer, new parents could draw down greater sums during the first two years after the birth of their child, enabling them to spend more time strengthening those all-important bonds without having to worry quite so much about money. Again the OBR could be tasked with informing the country about which benefits could be frontloaded, and how, for families with very young children.

At the other end of the scale, as children enter adulthood, thought should be given to how the means of financing the fees and living costs incurred by students and apprentices could be met by a reinvigorated form of social insurance specifically geared towards helping young people at the outset of their careers.

Objective 3: Healthy Homes for All
The country shall minimise the risk of homelessness and ensure that everybody has access to suitable accommodation that is affordable and of a decent standard.

The availability, affordability, and quality of our country's housing stock poses major ongoing risks to the welfare of the population, in addition to continued upward pressure on the welfare budget. The cessation of a private tenancy is now a leading cause of homelessness, stubbornly high rents continue to bloat the housing benefit bill and diminish renters' chances of saving for a deposit to buy their own home, and more than a quarter of all privately rented homes are in poor or unsafe condition.

We believe there would be great merit in an equivalent body to the NSC assessing, with support from the OBR, the potential impact on both our national welfare as well as the size of the welfare budget of introducing default tenancies of, say, three years for families renting privately, alongside what the Resolution Foundation has termed 'light touch' forms of rent control,[119] and legally enforceable minimum standards governing the quality of all rented accommodation. To give an idea of the potential effectiveness of preventative measures along these lines, an analysis commissioned by Crisis has found that, for every pound invested in the prevention and relief of homelessness, the country would gain a return of £2.80.[120]

As with student finance, we also believe that a reinvigorated social insurance mechanism, with support from banks and building societies, could open up opportunities for more people to buy their own homes. A strategic welfare review could set out how the Treasury might work with the financial services industry to develop new products, whereby an account holder could seek a mortgage even when they could not afford to pay an upfront deposit. The mortgage provider would know that, by moving from renting to buying, the account holder would gain enough in net income to pay back a deposit sum that it had notionally awarded them, as well as keeping good payment on their mortgage.

If mortgage providers wished for the Treasury to take on more of the upfront risk, one option could be to build up a new social insurance fund – perhaps using some of the proceeds from stamp duty, a fixed percentage from monthly mortgage repayments, or both – which covered all or part of an account holder's deposit.

Objective 4: A National Minimum of Health

The country shall ensure that anyone in need of health and social care services receives the highest possible standard of care, thereby eliminating as far as possible the existence of health inequalities in this country.

It was Beveridge who set out clearly the application of a national minimum to the health of the population, stating that 'the national minimum for every citizen today should include being well, being as well as science applied to prevention and cure of disease can make him'.[121] The enforcement of this aspect of the national minimum will, in the years ahead, rely heavily on an adequate funding settlement being reached, and a recalibration of services being achieved, for the NHS and social care.

The IFS and the Health Foundation undertook much legwork in the year that followed the 2017 general election – both to renew the public debate on the financing of health and social care, and to set out the options available to ministers.

The report that resulted from this exercise, entitled *Securing the future: funding health and social care to the 2030s*, estimated that: overall health spending is likely to need to rise by around 3.3 per cent each year over the next fifteen years, just to maintain current service levels; within the first five years, annual increases will need to be as high as 4 per cent just to maintain current service levels and address the backlogs caused by previous funding restrictions; and an improved NHS could require annual funding increases of 4 per cent over the next fifteen years, increasing to 5 per cent within the first five years. This fifteen-year settlement would increase health spending as a proportion of national income from 7.3 per cent today, to 9.9 per cent in 2033–34; by 2033–34 there will be 4.4 million more people aged sixty-five and over, and 1.3 million aged eighty-five and over; over the next fifteen years spending in acute hospitals to treat people with chronic disease will need to more than double to meet growing levels of need; over that same period, the NHS in England is likely to require 64,000 additional hospital doctors and 171,000 additional nurses, while social care will require half a million more members of staff; and for each person treated in hospital, the cost of their drugs will increase by 5.5 per cent each year.[122]

Under the funding plans announced by the Prime Minister in June 2018, as a seventieth birthday gift to the NHS, health spending will grow in real terms by 3.6 per cent in 2019–20, 3.6 per cent in 2020–21, 3.1 per cent in 2021–22, 3.1 per cent in 2022–23, and 3.4 per cent in 2023–24. The Health Foundation and The King's Fund project growth in social care expenditure of just 2.1 per cent a year for the foreseeable future.[123]

Even under the Prime Minister's plans, the NHS in England will register a gap in funding of £3.8 billion in 2020–21.[124] That year's gap in funding for social care will be £1.5 billion, resulting in a total health and social care funding deficit of £5.3 billion.[125] That deficit arises in respect of the funding required to maintain existing service standards, let alone improve them. The Health Foundation and The King's Fund estimate that, in social care, restoring the levels of service and eligibility that existed in 2009–10 would widen that deficit by £6.5 billion.[126]

In taking forward the IFS and Health Foundation's conclusions that 'sustained increases in health and care spending will require increased revenues from somewhere', 'if we want even to maintain health and social care provision at current levels, taxes will have to rise', and 'it is hard to imagine raising this kind of money without increases in at least one of the three biggest taxes', we advocate an immediate £0.01 increase in National Insurance contributions which would raise in excess of £10 billion each year. This would both meet the immediate deficit in health and social care and pave the way for improvements in service levels.

But it would be a pity if the transformative opportunities that come with Brexit were not seized upon, through an equivalent body to the NSC, to begin to recast how the NHS and social care are financed; incorporate both the NHS and social care services into a more comprehensive health package; clearly earmark and deliver any increased expenditure to a combined health and social care budget; and establish a new governance arrangement between the electorate, health and social care services, and the government.

The longer-term reform we wish to advocate consists of a National Health and Social Care Service; a National Health and Social Care Mutual that would undertake key functions with the service and report to the NSC-equivalent body tasked with driving through a strategic welfare review; and a progressive, hypothecated National Insurance base that would fund the new service.

The main functions of the mutual would be to ensure that the funds allocated to the service were fully received, and begin a dialogue with the service on how best improvements in the delivery of care to patients can be achieved, so that the best possible value is obtained for each pound of National Insurance contributions.

The mutual would work with the existing services – the last thing health and social care services need is somebody to throw all the pieces up into the air again. In the longer term, the mutual would lead a debate on the future shape of a service that is not in a financial crisis, and take on a similar role to the OBR, or join forces, in drawing upon current trends to forecast the likely patterns of demand for health and social care, and the necessary levels of expenditure to meet that level of demand.

Its forecasts should be used to launch a dialogue with the public on the size of contributions that will be required to finance health and social care and to meet the nation's expectations of the service.

Equally important will be to conduct wherever possible a conversation with the mutual membership on the size of the increase in contributions that will be required if the current rules of accessibility, the embracing of new drugs and technology, and the maintenance and extension of new forms of surgery are to continue to be part of the new services menu. Membership will consist of all UK-born members of the public who are included within the National Insurance system, people who were born outside the UK but who have built up a set period of National Insurance contributions, and the service's own staff.

In the first instance, the governing trustees of the mutual should be appointed by the equivalent body to the NSC tasked with driving through the strategic welfare review. Eventually, the mutual should be governed by trustees who are elected by its membership and would include a representative from the service's staff. The mutual would mark a major change in what is regarded as 'governance' in this country.

It is not only our governance models that are in need of major change. In ensuring that the welfare budget is set at a level that is affordable to taxpayers both today and in the long run, negotiations on our post-Brexit contract will also need to centre upon the extent to which new sources of revenue are required, or existing items of expenditure are to be reallocated, if increases in the welfare budget are to be delivered with the grain of taxpayers' sense of justice.

It would be rational in a twenty-first century world to tax sources of wealth, such as inheritance, but Britain does not yet seem to agree.

Wealth inequality has increased since the 1980s, with the share of total wealth owned by the top 1 per cent rising from 15 per cent in 1984 to 20–22 per cent by 2013. The increase in wealth concentration in the last four decades is very much a phenomenon confined to the top 0.5 per cent, and, in particular, to the top 0.1 per cent, whose share of total wealth doubled from 4.5 per cent to 9 per cent between 1984 and 2013.[127]

How might the debate begin to be recast over the shape of our tax base, so that lower paid taxpayers can receive the greatest possible protection from any additional revenue-raising measures in the years ahead? Several potential options, as follows, are worthy of further consideration in a strategic welfare review.

Flat-rate pensions tax relief – Compared with the current system, in which tax relief on contributions is at the individual's marginal rate, a 25 per cent flat tax relief on private pension contributions could have saved the government £3.7 billion in 2018. A flat rate of 20 per cent could have saved £9.4 billion.[128]

A flat rate of 25 per cent would also have increased the proportion of basic rate taxpayers benefitting from tax relief, from 35 per cent to 55 per cent. Only 45 per cent of the gains would thereby go to higher and additional rate taxpayers.

Pensioners' National Insurance – HMRC currently estimates that the National Insurance exemption for people of pensionable age costs around £950 million in contributions to the government.

Pensions Triple Lock – According to the House of Commons Library, had the State Pension been 'double locked' against Consumer Price Index inflation and average earnings between 2012–13 and 2015–16, annual expenditure might have been around £1 billion less in 2015–16 than was, in reality, the case under the Triple Lock.

A turnover tax on multinational companies – The government is exploring the option of a tax on the turnover of multinational companies, to capture more adequately the sources from which their value is generated. The *Financial Times* has reported in recent years on how eBay paid £1.6 million in UK corporation tax in 2016, on at least £200 million of revenues (although its US filings suggest revenues of over £1 billion),[129] and how Amazon's warehouse and logistics division was owed money by HMRC, despite generating more than £1 billion of revenues in 2016. Meanwhile, Facebook paid £2.6 million of corporation tax on revenues of £842.4 million in 2016, and Google, which recorded £1 billion of revenues in Britain from 2015–16, paid tax of £25.1 million.

As Rana Foroohar notes, tax 'optimisation', as the offshoring of assets by multinational companies is euphemistically known, has long been one of the sore points of globalisation.

Capital moves easily across borders, which means that large companies that are able to shift profits to low-tax jurisdictions benefit disproportionately from the system.[130] One option for raising additional revenues here could be to apply a turnover tax only to firms above a certain size, or with a certain market share.

Personal wealth tax – Variations of a wealth tax have been agonised over by successive generations of reformers. A most recent incarnation is Nick Donovan's proposal for a one-off levy on long-term residents in this country with net passive wealth over £10 million, with a second, higher rate charged on net wealth that exceeds a threshold of £20 million. 'High risk' taxpayers – those who have moved assets offshore or used domestic tax avoidance schemes, or non-doms who pay the remittance basis charge – would be required to undergo a full, stringent valuation exercise.[131] Previous one-off levies include Stafford Cripps' 'special contribution', Roy Jenkins' 'special charge', and Gordon Brown's windfall tax on the excess profits of the privatised utilities.

Taxation of property – Reformers have similarly been seeking to grapple with the longstanding failure of the Council Tax system to reflect the true value of properties, particularly towards the top end of the scale, over the past three decades.

The major distortion within the property and wealth tax

regime is in Council Tax. The current system means that, overall, property and wealth held by households living in larger and more expensive properties is undertaxed while households in smaller and cheaper properties are overtaxed. No surprise, therefore, that calls for it to be replaced with a more fitting and equitable alternative are becoming louder and more frequent.

A most recent proposal, put forward by the Resolution Foundation, would involve replacing Council Tax with two different taxes.[132] First, a proportional tax of 0.5 per cent on the reassessed value of a property would raise an additional £1.6 billion a year. 17 million households would pay less and 9.2 million would pay more. Second, a flat tax of 1 per cent on the value of a property, above a £100,000 allowance per property, would raise an additional £8.6 billion a year. 15.2 million households would pay more and 10.9 million would pay less.

We have attempted here to open up the debate on the terms of a social contract to govern the welfare budget in post-Brexit Britain, as well as to spell out some of the themes that could be covered in an initial strategic welfare review – the pursuit of full employment across the whole country; a fully functioning safety net for the most vulnerable; the equalisation of children's life chances; the provision of stable, affordable, and decent accommodation for all of our citizens; and a comprehensive service that meets our health and care needs for the next generation.

Conclusion

The immediate adoption of a strategic welfare review is required to convert the Prime Minister's multi-year funding plan for the NHS into a meaningful way of securing our country's welfare for the next generation.

The regular appearance of such a review on the political scene, based on the development of the OBR's work in forecasting and analysing future risks, will enable the government to spell out to the country what those risks are, the reforms that are necessary if we are to counter them, the costs of doing so, and the alternative ways of meeting these costs.

In its absence, the government will carry on struggling both to reach a satisfactory settlement with taxpayers to pay for existing service levels, as well as to factor in bold ideas for what type of society people want after Brexit.

Let us take as an example how the Prime Minister's plan for the NHS will be paid for. Will the money come from other parts of the welfare, policing, or defence budgets? If additional contributions are sought from taxpayers, will they be sought mainly from those who are more, or less, fortunate? How will the burden be shared by those above and below the retirement age, and by companies and individuals? And will additional monies be yielded from assets or incomes?

Moreover, how will the new monies link in with social care and other parts of the welfare budget, such as housing and the Foundation Years that are similarly crucial to the longer-term health and wellbeing of the population?

And what level of service can the public expect in return for the additional funding committed by the Prime Minister? Are taxpayers content with a mere continuation of existing levels of service, or do they expect certain improvements in return for additional sums? If so, how will the NHS be reconfigured to deliver those improvements, and how will the government report back to taxpayers on whether they have been delivered? Will the additional monies represent yet another patching up exercise if there is no accompanying adequate settlement for social care? On first glance, the plan will struggle to maintain even existing levels of service, let alone deliver any major improvements in the quality and coverage of health and social care.

One-off reviews, as we have shown, tend not to translate into meaningful, rounded, and long-lasting solutions. This is much to the detriment of the objectives sought by taxpayers from different parts of the welfare budget, with one consequence being the bearing of ever greater risks by the most vulnerable individuals in our country.

Only a strategic welfare review that seeks constantly to analyse these matters in the round, and to lock in a broad coalition of interests behind the changing shape of the welfare budget and its objectives, is able to forge a satisfactory settlement between the government and taxpayers on each of these crucial questions.

This is the political innovation that will set our country on the path towards the common good after Brexit.

Notes

1   Sir William Beveridge, *Social Insurance and Allied Services* (London: HM Stationery Office, 1942): p. 6

2   Bentley Gilbert, *The Evolution of National Insurance in Great Britain: The Origins of the Welfare State* (London: Michael Joseph, 1966)

3   In a YouGov poll recording which budgets voters most wanted to protect or cut conducted by Dr Joel Rogers de Waal in October 2014, defence spending sat roughly in the middle. Further polling for YouGov conducted by William Jordan in 2015 found that, up against other spending priorities, one in four voters named defence as one of three areas that should be protected from cuts, putting it level with pensions (27 per cent) but behind crime and policing (35 per cent), education and schools (50 per cent), and the National Health Service (79 per cent).

4   The National Living Wage is the statutory minimum wage for employees aged 25 and over.

5   Jonathan Cribb, Agnes Norris Keiller, and Tom Waters, *Living standards, poverty and inequality in the UK: 2018* (London: The Institute for Fiscal Studies, 2018): p. 95

6   John Vaizey, *The Costs of Education* (London: Allen and Unwin, 1958)

7   *Central Organisation for Defence*, Cmd. 476 (London: HM Stationery Office, 1958): p. 3

8   Peter Hennessy, *Distilling the Frenzy: Writing the History of One's Own Times* (London: Biteback Publishing, 2013): p. 28

9   National Audit Office, *Ministry of Defence: The Equipment Plan 2017 to 2027* (January 2018)

10 We invite the reader for one moment to apply the following extracts from *National Security Capability Review* (March 2018), as well as the logic behind them, to an equivalent exercise covering the welfare budget: 'Last year, we commissioned the National Security Capability Review to establish how best we can apply our national security apparatus to address the increasing and diversifying threats to our country and to our way of life.'; 'Since the [Cameron government's review] was published, threats have continued to intensify and evolve and we face a range of complex challenges at home and overseas.'; 'Our national security is conditional [...] on our ability to mobilise most effectively the full range of our capabilities in concert to respond to the challenges we face. So as this report sets out, we have agreed a new approach to the orchestration of our national security capabilities.'; 'Every part of our

government and every one of our agencies has its part to play.'; 'We must identify the most effective and efficient combination of ways to achieve the government's objectives over the long term [...] to do all this we need robust analysis, drawing on all sources of information and data from both within government and outside.'; '[Having identified the specific challenges] we remain committed to grow defence spending by at least 0.5 per cent above inflation each year to 2020/21; [...] spend 0.7 per cent of GNI on Official Development Assistance [...]; increase counter-terrorism spending by over 30 per cent over the Spending Review period; and grow the Single Intelligence Account budget by 18 per cent in real terms.'; 'We remain on track to recruit and train over 1,900 additional security and intelligence staff across the agencies to respond to, and deter, those behind the increasing international terrorist, cyber and global threats.'; 'The NSC was created in 2010 to oversee and co-ordinate all aspects of our national security as part of collective cabinet decision-making.'; 'The NSC will take stock each year of the UK's positioning on national security in terms of resilience, threats and opportunities to take decision about strategic prioritisation.'; 'For each of its priorities, the NSC will consider UK interests and objectives, the situation we face and the outlook, and then the wider national or international strategy to decide how to make a catalytic contribution, considering our full range of capabilities. The NSC's ambition must match the resources committed so that we pursue realistic objectives and prioritise scarce resources where they can make most difference as part of our collective approach.'; 'We have commissioned the Modernising Defence Programme, led by the Ministry of Defence, working with Cabinet Office and across government, which will report to the Prime Minister, Chancellor of the Exchequer and Defence Secretary. It is identifying how we can deliver better military capability and better value for money to make a full and enduringly sustainable contribution to national security and prosperity.'

11 HM Government, *National Security Capability Review* (March 2018): p. 15

12 HM Government, *National Security Strategy and Strategic Defence and Security Review 2015: A Secure and Prosperous United Kingdom* (November 2015): p. 40

13 HM Government, *National Security Strategy and Strategic Defence and Security Review 2015: A Secure and Prosperous United Kingdom* (November 2015): p. 6

14 HM Government, *National Security Strategy and Strategic Defence and Security Review 2015: A Secure and Prosperous United Kingdom* (November 2015): p. 64

15 Nick Davies, Lucy Campbell, and Chris McNulty, *How to fix the funding of health and social care* (Institute for Government, 2018): p. 14

16 John Veit-Wilson, 'The National Assistance Board and the 'Rediscovery' of Poverty', in H. Fawcett and R. Lowe (eds.), *Welfare Policy in Britain: The Road from 1945* (Basingstoke: Macmillan, 1999): pp. 116–157

17 One group, chaired by Allan Beard, considered the scale rates for children; another, chaired by Robert Windsor, looked at the adult scale rates.

18 The 'six principles of social insurance' were: flat rate of subsistence benefit; flat rate of contribution; unification of administrative responsibility; adequacy of benefit; comprehensiveness; and classification.

19 The 'three assumptions' were: cash allowances for families with children; a comprehensive health service; and the maintenance of full employment.

20 W.H. Beveridge, *Social Insurance and Allied Services*, Cmd. 6404 (London: HM Stationery Office, 1942): p. 12

21 'Appendix A: Finance of the Proposals of the Report Relating to Social Insurance and Security Benefits – Memorandum by the Government Actuary', in W.H. Beveridge, *Social Insurance and Allied Services*, Cmd. 6404 (London: HM Stationery Office, 1942): p. 210

22 *War Cabinet – Social Insurances and Allied Services: Summary of Report by Sir William Beveridge*, W.P. (42) 547 (25 November 1942): p. 3

23 National Audit Office, *Rolling out Universal Credit* (15 June 2018): p. 38

24 National Audit Office, *Tackling problem debt* (6 September 2018)

25 *War Cabinet – Social Insurances and Allied Services: Summary of Report by Sir William Beveridge*, W.P. (42) 547 (25 November 1942): p. 2

26 Four of which – those of 1954 (Phillips), 1978 (DHSS), 1984 (Fowler), and 1993 (Lilley) – were listed by Steven Kennedy and Wendy Wilson, House of Commons Library, in 'Strategic reviews: health, housing and social security', commissioned by Frank Field, 30 August 2017. The other two are the Turner Commission and the Cridland Review.

27 *Report of the Committee on the Economic and Financial Problems of the Provision for Old Age*, Cmd. 9333 (London: HM Stationery Office, 1954): pp. 78–79

28 Consider, for example, how the report outlined: 'The subject of our Enquiry has been the economic and financial problems which arise from the prospect of a steady and substantial increase in the number of old persons as against a working population remaining roughly constant. Primarily, these problems are

concerned with the provision of income for the old,
not only under the schemes of National Insurance
and National Assistance but also under occupational
pension schemes and other forms of private provision.
Although we have devoted most our attention to this
aspect, we have also considered certain services which
are needed or are used by old people, such as hospital
treatment, residential accommodation and domiciliary
services. The old are not the only people who need or
use these services but they claim a large, and in some
respects specialised share, and the scale of provision will
be influenced by the increasing number of old people in
the population.'

29   Department of Social Security, *The Growth of Social
      Security* (London: HM Stationery Office, 1993): p. 2

30   Department of Social Security, *The Growth of Social
      Security* (London: HM Stationery Office, 1993): p. 10

31   The Triple Lock on state pension increases was
      introduced by the Coalition Government, to link
      annual increases to the highest of either earnings
      increases, inflation increase, or 2.5 per cent.

32   *Independent Review of the State Pension Age: Smoothing
      the Transition* (2017): p. 16

33   Peter Taylor-Gooby, *The Double Crisis of the Welfare
      State and What We Can Do About It* (Basingstoke:
      Palgrave Macmillan, 2013): p. xi

34 *Fairer Care Funding: The Report of the Commission on Funding of Care and Support: Volume 1* (2011): p. 5

35 *Fairer Care Funding: The Report of the Commission on Funding of Care and Support: Volume 1* (2011): p. 5

36 Commission on the Future of Health and Social Care in England, *A new settlement for health and social care: Final report* (King's Fund, 2014): p. vi

37 Greg Hurst, 'Elderly face impossible search for a care home', *The Times* (4 October 2017): p. 27

38 Commission on the Future of Health and Social Care in England, *A new settlement for health and social care: Final report* (King's Fund, 2014): p. vii

39 Commission on the Future of Health and Social Care in England, *A new settlement for health and social care: Final report* (King's Fund, 2014): p. 33

40 Competition and Markets Authority, *Care homes market study: Final report* (2017)

41 Andrew Kingston et al., 'Is late-life dependency increasing or not? A comparison of the Cognitive Function and Ageing Studies' (*The Lancet*, Vol. 390, 2017): p. 1681

42 Health and Social Care Committee and Housing, Communities and Local Government Committee, 'Long-term funding of adult social care: First joint report of session 2017–19' (London: The Stationery Office, 2018)

43 The 'six principles' are: providing high-quality care; considering working-age adults as well as older people; ensuring fairness on the 'who and how' we pay for social care, including between the generations; aspiring over time towards universal access to personal care free at the point of delivery; risk pooling – protecting people from catastrophic costs, and protecting a greater portion of their savings and assets; and 'earmarking' of contributions to maintain public support.

44 The 'seven principles' are: quality; whole-person integrated care; control; workforce; supporting families and carers; a sustainable funding model supported by a diverse, vibrant, and stable market; and security for all.

45 House of Lords Select Committee on the Long-Term Sustainability of the NHS, Oral Evidence, Tuesday 13 December 2016 (QQ278-285)

46 Anita Charlesworth and Paul Johnson (eds.), *Securing the future: funding health and social care to the 2030s* (London: Institute for Fiscal Studies, and The Health Foundation, June 2018): p. ii

47 Brian Abel-Smith and Richard Titmuss, *The Cost of the National Health Service* (Cambridge: Cambridge University Press, 1956)

48 Charles Webster, *The National Health Service: A Political History*, 2nd ed., (Oxford: Oxford University Press, 2002): p. 32

49   *Report of the Committee of Inquiry into the Cost of the National Health Service*, Cmd. 9663 (London, HM Stationery Office, 1956).

50   Webster, *The National Health Service*, p. 33. This quote is taken from the second edition of Webster's book, which was published in 2002, and cited in a House of Commons Library analysis written by Wendy Wilson and Steven Kennedy.

51   NHS England, *Five Year Forward View* (October 2014): p. 36

52   Webster, *The National Health Service*, pp. 232–234

53   Ed Balls, *Speaking Out: Lessons in Life and Politics* (London: Hutchinson, 2016): p. 97

54   Ed Balls, *Speaking Out: Lessons in Life and Politics* (London: Hutchinson, 2016): p. 98

55   Derek Wanless, *Securing Our Future Health: Taking a Long Term View. Interim Report*, 2001

56   Derek Wanless, *Securing Our Future Health: Taking a Long Term View. A Final Report*, 2002

57   Ed Balls, *Speaking Out: Lessons in Life and Politics* (London: Hutchinson, 2016): p. 102

58   Anita Charlesworth and Paul Johnson (eds.), *Securing the future: funding health and social care to the 2030s* (London: Institute for Fiscal Studies, and The Health Foundation, June 2018): p. x

59   Derek Wanless, *Securing Good Care for Older People* (The King's Fund, 2006): p. xxi

60   House of Lords Select Committee on the Long-term Sustainability of the NHS, report of 2016–17 (2017): pp. 3–7

61   The Chancellor of the Exchequer, HC Deb 22 June 2010, vol 512, col 166–167

62   The Chancellor of the Exchequer, HC Deb 20 October 2010, vol 516, col 949–965

63   Anita Charlesworth and Paul Johnson (eds.), *Securing the future: funding health and social care to the 2030s* (London: Institute for Fiscal Studies, and The Health Foundation, June 2018): p. iii

64   OBR, *Economic and Fiscal Outlook* (March 2018): p. 11

65   In fact, changes in the personal allowance help those on higher incomes the most.

66   Crisis, *Homelessness projections: Core homelessness in Great Britain*, August 2017, https://www.crisis.org.uk/media/237582/crisis_homelessness_projections_2017.pdf

67   Jonathan Cribb, Agnes Norris Keiller, and Tom Waters, *Living standards, poverty and inequality in the UK: 2018* (London: The Institute for Fiscal Studies, 2018): p. 95

68   Lord Darzi, *The Lord Darzi Review of Health and Care: Interim Report* (IPPR, April 2018)

69   Anita Charlesworth and Paul Johnson (eds.), *Securing the future: funding health and social care to the 2030s* (London: Institute for Fiscal Studies, and The Health Foundation, June 2018): p. iv

70   Robert J. Myers, *Expansionism in Social Insurance* (London: The Institute of Economic Affairs, 1970): pp. 30–31

71   Paul Johnson, *High levels of income for current retirees shouldn't blind us to future challenges* (Institute for Fiscal Studies: 20 October 2015), https://www.ifs.org.uk/publications/8026

72   Institute for Fiscal Studies, *Living standards, poverty and inequality in the UK 2016*, p. 9

73   Institute for Fiscal Studies, *Living standards, poverty and inequality in the UK 2016*, p. 59

74   These data come from an analysis conducted by Philip Brien, Richard Keen, and Rachael Harker in the House of Commons Library, commissioned by Frank Field in March 2018.

75   Elaine Kelly, Tom Lee, Luke Sibieta, and Tom Waters, *Public Spending on Children in England: 2000 to 2020* (Children's Commissioner and the Institute for Fiscal Studies, 2018): p. 51

76   Child Poverty Action Group, *UK child poverty gaps still increasing* (May 2018), http://www.cpag.org.uk/sites/

default/files/uploads/UK%20child%20poverty%20
gaps%20increasing%20again.pdf

77   National Audit Office, *Discharging older patients from
     hospital* (May 2016): p. 7

78   Simon Nicol, Mike Roys, Helen Garrett, and BRE,
     The cost of poor housing to the NHS (Building Research
     Establishment, 2015)

79   All-Party Parliamentary Group on Hunger, *Hidden
     hunger and malnutrition in the elderly* (January 2018):
     p. 4

80   David Buck and David Maguire, *Inequalities in life
     expectancy: Changes over time and implications for policy*
     (The King's Fund, 2015)

81   Duncan Gallie and Carolyn Vogler, 'Labour Market
     Deprivation, Welfare, and Collectivism', in Duncan
     Gallie, Catherine Marsh, and Carolyn Vogler (eds.),
     Social Change and the Experience of Unemployment
     (Oxford: Oxford University Press, 1994): pp. 299–336

82   The Marmot Review, *Fair Society, Healthy Lives*
     (Institute of Health Equity, 2010): p. 68

83   The Marmot Review, *Fair Society, Healthy Lives*
     (Institute of Health Equity, 2010): p. 69

84   The Marmot Review, *Fair Society, Healthy Lives*
     (Institute of Health Equity, 2010): p. 70

85   Office for National Statistics, *UK labour market:
     September 2018*, p. 23

86 World Economic Forum, *The Global Risks Report 2017: 12th Edition* (2017): pp. 35–37

87 A.B. Atkinson, *Poverty and social security* (Hemel Hempstead: Harvester Wheatsheaf, 1989): p. 93

88 Tony Atkinson, 'Social Policy: Looking Backward and Looking Forward', in *Social Policy Futures: Wreckage, Resilience or Renewal – Report of proceedings of the Department of Social Policy's 100th Anniversary Colloquium, 7th December 2012* (London: LSE Academic Publishing, 2015): p. 85

89 Nicholas Timmins, *The Five Giants: A Biography of the Welfare State – Third Edition* (London: William Collins, 2017): p. 707

90 Matthew Goodwin and Oliver Heath, *Brexit vote explained: poverty, low skills and lack of opportunities* (Joseph Rowntree Foundation, 2016)

91 Theresa May, *Statement from the new Prime Minister Theresa May* (GOV.UK: 13 July 2016), https://www.gov.uk/government/speeches/statement-from-the-new-prime-minister-theresa-may

92 Sidney Webb, *National Finance and a Levy on Capital: Fabian Tract 188* (London: The Fabian Society, 1919): p. 9

93 Lord Darzi, *The Lord Darzi Review of Health and Care: Interim Report* (IPPR, April 2018): p. 42

94 Brian Rodgers, *The Battle Against Poverty, Volume 2: Towards a Welfare State* (London: Routledge and Kegan Paul, 1969): p. 28

95 Charter for Budget Responsibility (HM Treasury, 23 November 2016)

96 OBR, *Welfare trends report* (October 2016): p. 5

97 OBR, *Welfare trends report* (October 2016): p. 6

98 OBR, *Fiscal sustainability report* (January 2017): p. 3

99 OBR, *Fiscal sustainability report* (January 2017): p. 7

100 OBR, *Fiscal sustainability report* (January 2017): p. 51

101 OBR, *Fiscal sustainability report* (January 2017): p. 61

102 OBR, *Fiscal sustainability report* (January 2017): p. 90

103 Roger Harding, *A backlash against austerity?* (British Social Attitudes), http://www.bsa.natcen.ac.uk/latest-report/british-social-attitudes-34/key-findings/a-backlash-against-austerity.aspx

104 *King's Fund releases new analysis of British Social Attitudes data on NHS funding* (NatCen, 12 April 2018), http://www.natcen.ac.uk/news-media/latest-news/2018/march/kings-fund-releases-new-analysis-of-british-social-attitudes-data-on-nhs-funding/

105 *Daily Mirror NHS Poll – June 2018* (ComRes, 6 June 2018), http://www.comresglobal.com/polls/daily-mirror-nhs-poll/

106 Sophie Gaston, *Citizens' Voices: Insights from focus groups conducted in England for the project 'At Home in One's Past'* (Demos, 2018): p. 6

107 Eleanor Taylor et al., *Social and political attitudes of people on low incomes: 2017 report* (NatCen, 2017): p. 15

108 Peter Taylor-Gooby, *The Double Crisis of the Welfare State and What We Can Do About It* (Basingstoke: Palgrave Macmillan, 2013): p. 103

109 The National Committee for the Prevention of Destitution, *The Case for the National Minimum* (London, 1913)

110 Beatrice Webb, *Our Partnership*, Barbara Drake and Margaret Cole (eds.) (London: Longmans, Green and Co., 1948): p. 418

111 Winston Churchill, 'Liberalism and Socialism', speech delivered at St Andrew's Hall, Glasgow, on 11 October 1906

112 H.H. Asquith, 'Liberal Leader's Speech', speech delivered in Manchester in 1918

113 G.D.H. Cole, *Fabian Socialism* (London: George Allen & Unwin, 1943): p. 31

114 W.H. Beveridge, 'Social Security and Social Policy', in *The Pillars of Security and other War-Time Essays and Addresses* (London: George Allen & Unwin, 1943): p. 143

115 Jane Waldfogel and Elizabeth Washbrook, 'Early years policy' (*Child Development Research*, 2011): p. 5; and Jane Waldfogel and Elizabeth Washbrook, *Low income and early cognitive development in the UK – A Report for the Sutton Trust* (2010): p. 18

116 Edward Melhuish, Julian Gardiner, and Stephen Morris, *Study of Early Education and Development (SEED): Impact Study on Early Education Use and Child Outcomes up to Age Three* (Department for Education, 2017): p. 54

117 Edward Melhuish and Julian Gardner, *Study of Early Education and Development (SEED): Impact Study on Early Education Use and Child Outcomes up to age four years* (Department for Education, 2018): pp. 94–95

118 The Marmot Review, *Fair Society, Healthy Lives* (Institute of Health Equity, 2010): pp. 97–98

119 Resolution Foundation, *A New Generational Contract: The final report of the Intergenerational Commission* (May 2018): p. 17

120 PwC, *Assessing the costs and benefits of Crisis' plan to end homelessness* (June 2018)

121 W.H. Beveridge, 'Plan for Social Security', in *The Pillars of Security and other War-Time Essays and Addresses* (London: George Allen & Unwin, 1943): p. 57

122 Anita Charlesworth and Paul Johnson (eds.), *Securing the future: funding health and social care to the*

2030s (Institute for Fiscal Studies, and The Health Foundation, June 2018)

123 Simon Bottery, Michael Varrow, Ruth Thorlby, and Dan Wellings, *A fork in the road: Next steps for social care funding reform* (The Health Foundation and The King's Fund, 2018)

124 House of Commons Library analysis from Rachael Harker, commissioned by Frank Field MP

125 Simon Bottery, Michael Varrow, Ruth Thorlby, and Dan Wellings, *A fork in the road: Next steps for social care funding reform* (The Health Foundation and The King's Fund, 2018): p. 3

126 Simon Bottery, Michael Varrow, Ruth Thorlby, and Dan Wellings, *A fork in the road: Next steps for social care funding reform* (The Health Foundation and The King's Fund, 2018): p. 16

127 Facundo Alvaredo et al., *World Inequality Report 2018* (World Inequality Lab, 2017): p. 241

128 Pensions Policy Institute, *Future trends in pensions tax relief* (July 2016): p. 10

129 Madison Marriage and Aliya Ram, *Why the UK is getting tough on Big Tech's tax* (Financial Times, 27 February 2018), https://www.ft.com/content/c10e59d2-1ae6-11e8-aaca-4574d7dabfb6

130 Rana Foroohar, *The need for a fair means of digital taxation increases* (Financial Times, 28 February 2018),

https://www.ft.com/content/6f2b6c9c-1b2f-11e8-aaca-4574d7dabfb6

131 Nick Donovan, *A Unique Contribution* (Fabian Society, 2017)

132 Adam Corlett and Laura Gardiner, *Home Affairs: Options for reforming property taxation* (Resolution Foundation, 2018): p. 45